MW01659500

NOTHING IS TOO GOOD TO BE TRUE!

7 STEPS To Personal Freedom & Creative Fulfillment

LEONA EVANS STEFANKO
AND CAROL KEEFER

ISA

INSTITUTE FOR SELF-AWARENESS, INC.
P. O. BOX 30131
PENSACOLA, FL 32503
(904) 435-0588

The names and circumstances of people used in case histories have been changed to protect their privacy.

 Published by Institute for Self-Awareness, Inc., P.O. Box 30131, Pensacola, FL 32503, 904/435-0588.

ISBN 0-9633732-0-X
Library Of Congress Catalog Number 92-73875

MANUFACTURED IN THE UNITED STATES OF AMERICA

Cover Art: Marilyn Nerad, Pensacola, FL
Cover Design: Alyce Robnett, Oklahoma City, OK
Typesetting: Type Designs, Pensacola, FL

This book is lovingly dedicated
to everyone who has a dream.
May this process reveal
your inherent goodness and power,
and guide you to the expression
of your deepest desires.

Acknowledgements

We are grateful to Esther Gilstrap,
Sophie & Gene Knowles,
Don Parker, and
the devoted congregation at
Unity of Gulf Breeze, Florida,
for their confidence
and loving support.

TABLE OF CONTENTS

— INTRODUCTION —

If you have ever set a goal and not reached it — if you have ever followed a dream and lost sight of it — if you have ever settled for less than you really want — this book is written for you!

No matter how many times you've tried and failed — no matter what others think you can or can't do — no matter how many self-help books you've bought and discarded as ineffective — the truth is that right now... right where you are... you have all that it takes to create a productive and successful life.

YOU CAN USE WHAT YOU ALREADY HAVE
TO GET WHAT YOU REALLY WANT!

We all know people who seem to lead charmed lives. "Everything they touch turns to gold," we say. These "successful" people know a secret — perhaps they know it consciously, perhaps they know it intuitively — but because of what they know, they are putting into practice a *specific process* that enables them to turn their dreams into reality.

IF THEY CAN DO IT, YOU CAN LEARN TO DO IT, TOO.

How Does The Process Work?

I did not invent this seven-step creative process. The process, itself, is a part of the natural order of creation. It is present every time a dream becomes a reality. It is absent in every case of failure. What I have done, is identify the process, and label the steps, so they can be used by anyone.

As a minister and spiritual counselor, I have seen literally hundreds of individuals all yearning to achieve their goals. Some succeeded, some did not! I have seen this phenomenon at work in my own life, as well. For years, I picked up every self-help book that promised to reveal the secrets of success. I applied the suggested techniques with all the dedication I could muster. Sometimes I succeeded, sometimes I didn't.

Why does this happen? How is it that hard work and dedication to a purpose only produce the desired results *sometimes* and not at other times? How can we go from feeling victimized by circumstances around us, to feeling as if we have some control over our lives? What is the secret ingredient that ensures a positive outcome every time we set a reasonable plan into action?

In an effort to respond to these questions, I took some of the many case histories from my experience and began to put them into two categories: those who had a goal or dream fulfilled, and those who had just as strong a goal and did *not* have it fulfilled.

During my research, a pattern began to emerge. In those cases where the goal was reached, there seemed to be a particular *process* that took place. It wasn't just one technique. It wasn't just goal-setting, or creative visualization, or possibility-thinking. Rather, it was a number of techniques, *used in a very specific order*, that produced a successful outcome.

When the effort was *not* successful, often some of the same techniques were used — but they were taken out-of-order, or there just weren't enough of them to bring about the desired results.

I became aware that there is a specific *process* through which things come into being. It begins the very first time we conceive an idea in our minds as a remote possibility. It continues through a gestation period, and finally emerges into manifestation.

> *THE RIGHT STEPS*
> *TAKEN IN THE RIGHT ORDER*
> *LEAD TO SUCCESS!*

What This Book Will Reveal To You.

As you work through this seven-step creative process, you will learn that true success is not accomplished by *changing* yourself, but by *becoming* yourself. You can enjoy a happier, healthier and more abundant life; and the only real change you need to make is in the way you *see* yourself.

> *YOU DON'T HAVE TO CHANGE YOURSELF,*
> *JUST "REINTERPRET" YOURSELF!*

When you know who you really are, you will understand that *you were created to fulfill yourself in a unique and purposeful way.* In other words... YOU WERE BORN TO SUCCEED AS ONLY YOU CAN!

Each of the seven chapters in this book is devoted to one of the seven steps in this creative process. These steps will teach you methods that will help you choose your goals and achieve them. You will be given practical applications of each step, self-knowledge tests, easy and entertaining exercises, and a wealth of ideas about how to apply these steps in every area of your life.

You'll learn how to free yourself from the limiting beliefs that invite failure; how to gain accurate self-knowledge, so you can choose goals that are right for you; how to develop a deep level of dedication to these goals that will assure success; how to prepare yourself for accomplishment; how to nurture yourself in the process of unfolding your potential; how to express yourself in a creative and fulfilling way; and how to relax and enjoy the good life you were meant to live.

OVERVIEW

Identify Your Personal Power!

More than 2,300 years ago, Plato spoke of philosopher kings as being those few individuals who had reached a place in life where they could spend most of their time contemplating and discussing their innermost thoughts and ideas.

These people were free from concerns about survival and could concentrate on their aesthetic needs: who they were, why they existed, and where they were going. Plato referred to this way of life as the ultimate leisure.

Things have changed quite a bit since Plato's time. Technology has advanced to the point where many of us have a good deal of leisure time. We, too, can be free to think and feel ... to become conscious of our identity and our purpose.

Life has become easier for most of us in many ways. We no longer must toil every waking hour just to put food on the table and clothes on our backs. However, the problems we face are still those of survival — but survival of another kind. We're now seeking to survive spiritually, mentally, and emotionally, above and beyond our material needs ... the survival of fulfillment.

Never before in the history of civilization have we been as conscious of the power and strength of the human spirit. Many people have overcome situations they once believed to be insurmountable. There are those who have been healed of diseases that were thought to be incurable. Evidence of our personal power is all around us.

THE QUESTION IS NOT "HOW DO WE GET THE POWER?" BUT, "HOW DO WE CULTIVATE THE POWER WE ALREADY HAVE?"

Most people believe that some sort of creative intelligence governs the universe. Throughout history, people have called it by many different names. What you call it is not important. The important thing to realize is that each of us is profoundly linked with that power, and we have only begun to explore the exciting dimensions of the human mind.

Why Most Self-Help Books Don't!

Many of us, in a time of so many possibilities, are not taking advantage of the wonderful opportunities to fulfill ourselves. Not because we haven't got what it takes, but because we don't know how to use it. Very often we are confused, rather than helped, by the tremendous number of self-help books available; all suggesting methods that can be used to effect transformation in our lives.

Many of these books contain so-called "steps" to this or that: A THREE STEP PLAN FOR SUCCESS... FIVE STEPS TO GREATER HAPPINESS... EIGHT STEPS TO A BETTER SELF-IMAGE. In reality, most of these "steps" are not steps at all. They don't build upon each other in a process. They're not progressive. They're simply points in a program; a method of dividing a book into sections; chapter headings that have little, if any, dependence on the success of the previous step.

Ask anyone who is part of a 12-step recovery program what kind of progress they would have made if they had started with step four or step seven. They all will tell you that the steps must be taken in order. They also will tell you that not one of the steps can be skipped. Each of the 12 steps must be worked — in the right order — for recovery to be effective. This is true of the creative process as well. All of the steps must be taken, and must be taken in the right order, if true and lasting change is to take place.

Knowledge Is Power

It's a given that change is possible. Yet for many people, things remain the same. Many have worked really hard at effecting change in their lives only to feel thwarted and frustrated; only to feel as though they are banging their heads against the wall; only to feel as though something is missing or something is wrong, or that perhaps they just don't have what it takes.

This is far from the truth! We all have what it takes. The problem is not lack of strength, or lack of power, or lack of will. The problem is lack of *knowledge* — of ourselves and of a creative process that is so powerful that, once we become aware of it, we can achieve virtually anything our heart desires.

> *IT'S NOT ABOUT WHAT WE DON'T "HAVE,"*
> *IT'S ABOUT WHAT WE DON'T "KNOW!"*

The Aha! Factor

It is said that there are no original ideas. But there certainly are new and different ways of applying old ideas. Ways that can make the difference between true transformation and simply another in a long list of disappointing efforts.

So while this book might not reveal startling new techniques for improving your life (although it might), and while you might already know, at some level, that there is power inherent within you (although perhaps you don't), what is very new and very different is that these techniques for transformation are going to be presented to you in such a way that they become a "process".

This means that it's not a question of which tool to use, or which one is better than another. It's a matter of *when* and *how* to implement them so that they are effective for you. It's not about whether or not to visualize your goals. It's about *when* to visualize. It's not about whether or not to prepare yourself. It's about *when* that activity can achieve optimum results in your life.

These steps will open a world of possibilities for you. You'll suddenly realize that you have options you never imagined. You'll gain an entirely new understanding of what it means to be a creative human being. You'll finally realize that you have choices.

That's the secret of these steps, and why they can help you achieve what you truly desire.

There is No Such Thing as The Impossible Dream!

Before you begin work on this seven-step creative process, you need to get really clear on one thing!

> *YOU WERE CREATED*
> *NOT ONLY WITH THE "DESIRE" TO FULFILL YOURSELF,*
> *BUT WITH ALL THE "EQUIPMENT" TO FULFILL YOURSELF.*

What you must do is interpret your innermost desires. Discover what they truly represent. You wouldn't have these longings if they weren't possible for you in some form or shape.

You can identify your deepest desires as creative needs ... needs that should not be squelched, or put down as impossible dreams ... needs that represent an inner longing to express yourself as you were created to be. Your purpose in life is one of growth and fulfillment of your God-given potential, and only you can live your dream!

YOU HAVE SOMETHING SPECIAL AND UNIQUELY "YOU" TO SHARE WITH THE WORLD!

As human beings, we are alike in many ways, but also very different. Just as there is one substance called snow, yet each snowflake is unique, so we, as individuals, form one body called humankind, yet each of us has a distinct and valuable perspective to share.

You Have Everything You Need!

You are like the tiny acorn that is equipped with all that it needs to become a giant oak tree. You have within you all that you need to experience wholeness on every level of your being.

You can stop looking outside yourself for the qualities you desire. They're already a part of your basic nature. You just need to find a way to *develop* and *express* them. These steps can help you do just that!

I suggest you read through this book entirely so you can see how the steps work together. Then, come back to each step in order. Work the exercises, and use the affirmations and visualizations. Soon you will begin to see the changes in your beliefs about yourself, and in the world around you.

This book will take you on an exciting journey of discovery. With the things you'll learn about yourself, through this seven step creative process, you're going to come to realize that **NOTHING IS TOO GOOD TO BE TRUE!**

STEP ONE

FREE YOURSELF

Before we can make a significant change in our lives, we must first believe that it is possible for us to do so.

"Man alone, of all the creatures of the earth, can change his own pattern. Man alone is the architect of his destiny. The greatest discovery of our generation is that human beings, by changing the inner attitudes of their minds, can change the outer aspects of their lives."

WILLIAM JAMES

When I was four years old, I decided to go into show business! It never occurred to me that I couldn't do it. Had I been older and wiser, more savvy about life and risks, I might have given some thought to the possibility of failure. I might have taken the advice of skeptics. I might even have lost confidence in my talents and skills. As it was, however, at that time in my life, I really had no reason to think that I couldn't experience my dreams — and so I set about doing just that!

When I was four years old, I was free! Free from the "shoulds" and "oughts" and limiting beliefs about myself that I would acquire as I grew older. Beliefs that, 28 years later, would keep me in a career that had stopped being fulfilling for me.

There came a time, later in my life, when my options seemed very limited. But, at the age of four, I had no difficulty seeing myself as worthy and capable of experiencing life in a creative and fulfilling way. I believed that my heart's desire was possible for me. Furthermore, I believed I was entitled to it.

Can you remember a time in your life when you were unaffected by the doubts and fears of the world around you? Do you remember feeling entitled to the best that life had to offer? There was a time when we all felt the freedom to dream dreams — to expect good things to come our way. What happened to change that?

Well, as we began to grow up, we developed some misconceptions and distorted beliefs about ourselves. These beliefs were by-products of our socialization. We were taught that it is wrong to be self-centered. We were encouraged to be more concerned with giving than receiving. We were told that wanting to get our own way was not nice. We were advised to practice moderation and not to call too much attention to ourselves.

Of course, there is nothing wrong with these lessons. They are necessary for us to learn, if we want to get along in the world. Unfortunately, many of us carried them too far. We learned not to expect too much out of life. We began to equate our hopes and desires with negative character traits. We began to suppress our individuality, and the freedom to follow our dreams slowly slipped away.

Finding The Freedom, Again!

This freedom can be regained, and *you* can do it! You can recapture the self-confidence and positive expectations that came so easily to you as a child; and support these open attitudes with the wisdom and maturity you have developed as an adult. Once you do this, you will experience an even greater freedom — one in which you will take responsibility for your own creative abilities, and nurture them into expression.

You can learn to become open to options that you thought were closed to you. You can become free to take the initiative in situations where you thought you had no control. You can come to believe that the desires of your heart will actually become a reality for you. Freeing yourself from limiting beliefs is the critical first step in our creative process.

BEFORE WE CAN BEGIN TO SET GOALS
AND FORMULATE A PLAN OF ACTION TO ACHIEVE THEM,
IT IS NECESSARY TO CHANGE SOME CORE BELIEFS
ABOUT WHO WE ARE,
AND WHAT WE ARE CAPABLE OF ACCOMPLISHING!

Are You Setting Goals or Setting Yourself Up?

Too many self-help books address goal-setting as the number one priority. I agree that goal-setting is vitally important, but before we can ever hope to achieve our goals, we need to know that we are worthy and deserving of the happiness we long for.

Unfortunately, many people who set goals are not mentally and emotionally ready to actually experience what they set out to achieve. As a result, their goals remain unfulfilled and their feelings of self-doubt and powerlessness continue to be reinforced. They may wish for something better, but they don't really take those wishes seriously.

Turning Your Daydreams into Road Maps!

Just wishing on a star or longing or yearning for something better isn't enough. We all have daydreams, but how often do we view them as practical or even possible for us?

In our minds, we tend to separate wishful thinking from what we believe is actually possible. This is one of the reasons why so many of us are frustrated in our attempts to accomplish our goals. We dream about living the good life, but the fact is, we don't really *expect* that our dreams will ever come true for us.

Our goals are not being attained for a very simple reason: *our thinking is limited, and our self-image is distorted.* Most of us simply don't see ourselves as worthy and deserving of the best that life has to offer, and we don't put ourselves into our dreams.

> *THERE IS TOO GREAT A GAP*
> *BETWEEN WHO WE WANT TO BE,*
> *AND WHO WE THINK WE ARE.*

As a result, our goal-setting becomes nothing more than a random list of "what ifs." Instead of using our dreams as the catalyst for great achievement, they become mere flights of fancy... without the power to get off the ground. We must learn to listen to our dreams and pay attention to our desires, for in them lie the secrets of our success and fulfillment.

Goal-setting is not just about wishing hard for what we want. It's about feeling the power behind our dreams, and knowing, at a gut level, that we have what it takes to do whatever we want to do! It's about feeling worthy and deserving of experiencing the best that life has to offer. Most importantly, it's about recognizing our deepest desires as our destiny, and taking them as seriously as we have ever taken anything in our lives!

> *OUR DREAMS REPRESENT*
> *THE CREATIVE URGE WITHIN US,*
> *TAPPING AT THE DOOR OF OUR MINDS*
> *ENCOURAGING US TO PAY ATTENTION!*

When we believe that our dreams are actually possible for us, we have taken the first step in the creative process. The lack of this conviction can sabotage even the most earnest efforts.

The Good Life is Optional!

As we learn to free ourselves we become open to new ways of doing things. Life is full of options! In any given situation, we always have a variety of ways and means to arrive at our chosen destination. Unfortunately, most of us are so locked into a single path, we become blinded to the number of options that are actually available to us at all times.

The story is told of a man who was imprisoned in the dungeon of a large castle. Twice a day, for 20 years, a guard came to the dungeon, opened the door, and gave the prisoner his meals. After the meal was eaten, the guard took the tray, closed the door, and left the prisoner alone in the dungeon. Finally, the 20 year sentence was completed. The prisoner eagerly looked forward to his freedom. The guard came down to the dungeon on the morning of the final day. The prisoner was standing at the door waiting for him.

"Quickly," said the prisoner, "unlock the door. I can hardly wait to be free again."

The guard looked at the prisoner and said, "Open it yourself. It was never locked."

This story illustrates that the prison in which we find ourselves is self-imposed. It's a mental and emotional prison that we unwittingly create as we accept limitations about ourselves and our environment. As we recognize that we have options, we begin to take charge of our own lives. It is through this freedom that we come to learn more of what we can do. The more capable and confident we feel, the more energized and excited we become about doing things.

The reason the prisoner never walked out the door before, was that he *assumed* it was locked.

A CLOSED DOOR IS NOT THE SAME AS A LOCKED DOOR. A CLOSED DOOR CAN BE OPENED!

One of the main reasons we get into our self-imposed prisons is that we make assumptions about the way things are. We make assumptions about what we can or can't do about them — and mostly it's about what we *can't* do.

ASSUMPTIONS CAN BLIND US TO OUR OPTIONS!

Many of us never even consider alternatives ... unless we are forced to do so. In many cases, we are driven to seek options only out of necessity ... when our actual survival is being threatened.

You Can Open The Door!

From the time I was a young child, I had always believed that I was born to be in show business. My goal was to work in musical theater. However, after a number of years of doing Broadway shows, regional theater, and summer stock, I began to realize there were many elements of my career that, not only did not bring me happiness, but that actually caused me a tremendous amount of pain and disappointment.

I had been a professional performer since I was four years old, and although my name was not exactly a household word, I had managed to work steadily (no mean feat in this business) and had achieved some prominence in my field. Unfortunately, the possibilities for work in the theater are extremely limited. At any given time, there are only so many roles available, and of these available roles, only certain "types" are sought.

I began to suffer a real identity crisis. I was always trying to look like ... sound like ... be like ... whatever the casting directors were looking for at the time. I was beginning to lose myself entirely.

My agent suggested I switch from theater to nightclubs. He felt that by doing my own singing act, I would have the opportunity to stop playing "other people" and start expressing my individuality.

Choosing my own songs and developing my own style sounded good to me, so I took his advice, and began putting the act together. I hired a vocal coach, a choreographer, and a musical arranger. We worked for months to perfect each number. Finally, I took the act on the road, and toured successfully for several years, in the U.S., Canada, Mexico, and the Far East. However, even though working on my own did solve some of my problems, it also gave me a whole set of new ones.

I was uncomfortable with the nightclub atmosphere. The frustrations of the business, the uncertainty, the constant travelling, the loneliness, and the absence of any family life and security, were beginning to take a toll. For the first time in my life, I began to think seriously about quitting.

Leaving show business was a frightening prospect. I didn't believe I could be happy doing anything else. I also knew I couldn't continue with things as they were. I felt trapped.

During this time, a record producer from Nashville heard me perform and offered me a contract. It appeared to be a great opportunity to stay in the business, yet get away from the constant travel and lifestyle I found so depressing. I decided to give show business one last chance.

My first release was a "single" of the then-popular song, "Feelings." It played frequently on a number of Easy-Listening stations throughout the country, and the record promoters pronounced it a success. The producer was encouraged and asked me to do an album using original songs by a new and talented composer. The songs were perfect for my singing style, and everyone at the studio was enthusiastic about the project.

However, just before my album was completed, an event took place that turned our world upside down. During one of our final recording sessions, the producer suffered a massive heart attack. Everyone was in a panic. I rushed to call for an ambulance while someone else performed CPR. Unfortunately, despite all our efforts, he died on the way to the hospital. His company, and my album, died with him.

I was numb - devastated. Not only had I lost a friend and mentor, but it appeared that my career had died, as well. I was so despondent that, for a couple of months, I did nothing but sit in my house and stare mindlessly at the TV. It was a genuine time of grief.

Finally, there came a time when I could no longer ignore the fact that I had food to buy and bills to pay. I realized that I needed to pull myself together and find a job.

In my deep depression, I could not view this experience as the freedom to exercise options. I saw it as the end of my dreams. I thought I would never be *special* again. I didn't think I would ever again be able to use my talents and skills or enjoy my work.

However, I really needed to support myself, so I looked through the yellow pages, found an employment agency, and made an appointment for that same afternoon.

The agency was located in a busy downtown area. I left my car in a nearby parking garage and walked to the building where the agency was located.

The beautiful, tree-lined street was hustling and bustling with people rushing in and out of office buildings. There was an excitement in the air, and my spirits began to rise.

After so many weeks of solitude and depression, it felt good to be out in the world again. By the time I arrived at my destination, I was feeling better than I had in a long time.

The offices of the employment agency were lovely — lots of glass, expensive furniture, and pleasant-looking people. I introduced myself to the smiling receptionist. She handed me a clipboard and asked me to complete the attached application.

As I read the application, my newly-elevated spirits began to sink. All of the questions concerned clerical skills. CLERICAL SKILLS! I didn't even know how to *type*! I was crushed. I don't know what I expected, but it was beginning to appear as though I had nothing of value to offer.

After staring at the application for a few minutes, I gave it back to the receptionist. The only thing I had filled out was my name and address.

She looked at the form and said, "Don't you have any office experience?"

"Not really," I replied, feeling somewhat embarrassed.

"Well," she asked, "what can you do."

"I can sing and dance," I answered, laughing nervously.

She gave me a patient smile. "I mean," she said, "in a business office."

"Well, actually ... not much of anything," I admitted, "but I really do need to work."

She asked what kind of job I was looking for. I thought for a moment, and suddenly I noticed there was no typewriter or adding machine on her desk. There were just a few papers and a telephone. "Yours!" I exclaimed. "I'm looking for a job just like yours!"

"Well," she laughed, "your timing couldn't be more perfect. I just gave my notice about an hour ago. This job is open."

She sent me to interview with the office manager, and I got the job. I was very grateful, because I knew it meant that I would survive financially, but I really didn't expect to enjoy it.

Pretty soon, however, I began to feel a certain pride in taking accurate messages and having my voice represent the company. I discovered that I had a talent for relating to the clients in an enthusiastic and positive way. I actually began to enjoy my job.

A few weeks after I started working, the owner of the company came by the office. He told me that he and the manager had been observing me. They thought I was bright, personable and articulate, and would make a good employment counselor. He offered me the promotion that same day.

My immediate reaction was fear. I still knew very little about office work. I wondered how I would find jobs for my applicants when I didn't even understand what skills the positions required. I just couldn't see myself being able to learn all I would need to know to be effective in the job. I had reconciled myself to my present position and the challenge of the new job seemed too great.

There was one aspect of being an employment counselor, however, that did interest me. It was a commissioned position. The possibility of making four to five times the amount I was earning as a receptionist was too great an opportunity to turn down. I was frightened, but I really needed the money, so I opened myself up to learning something new.

For the first few weeks, it felt as if I was on another planet. I began to wonder what I had gotten myself into. But I soon realized that being an employment counselor was very much like being a theatrical agent — only for office workers. That was a framework I could understand. I realized that everything I had ever wanted my agent to do for me, I could do for my applicants. I was enthusiastic in recommending them to prospective employers. I was able to find out things about them, support them, and nurture them in ways that empowered them with greater self-confidence.

It wasn't long before I realized that I was having a good time. I felt a real sense of accomplishment when my applicants would call me and say, "I just love this job. I never would have thought of applying for it on my own. Thanks for suggesting it." I was discovering that being an employment counselor could be rewarding in a variety of ways.

It afforded me a number of new opportunities, and verified for me that I was capable not only of existing, but of thriving, outside a theatrical environment. That was something I had never thought possible.

It didn't mean that I had to stay in that job forever, and I didn't; but it did mean that I had a whole series of options and opportunities that I never believed existed. I would never have recognized or taken advantage of these options had it not been absolutely necessary.

Who knew I could do more than perform? I certainly didn't — until I had to! Armed with this knowledge, I was much more confident when I made an even more drastic career change a few years later. By the time I made the decision to enter ministerial school, I had some evidence that my capabilities extended beyond my present experience. I had become open to other options in my life.

It is important to ask ourselves how many assumptions we make about who we are and what we're capable of doing. Many of us live much of our lives unconsciously — from a habit perspective. These habits can keep us from moving out of our present state of mind and into an expanded awareness of the world of possibilities.

Free Yourself To Be Yourself!

It is necessary to the achievement of any creative process that we begin by understanding this important fact:

WE ARE MORE THAN WE PRESENTLY BELIEVE OURSELVES TO BE

We are more capable and more powerful than we realize. In order to experience our true nature, we must learn to release some of our old, limiting beliefs.

Here's your first assignment. It's a simple one. It only requires that you consider a possibility. You don't even have to *believe* it right now. Simply *consider* that you are more than you presently believe yourself to be.

This statement might sound abstract, but within it is an entire world of possibilities. I think it's very important not to force yourself into accepting this idea too quickly. Just ask yourself to consider the possibility that within you is, not only the *desire*, but the *ability* to find a greater sense of peace and fulfillment in your life.

IT'S NOT ABOUT CHANGING YOURSELF.
IT'S ABOUT BEING YOURSELF.

It's about freeing yourself to become who you really are.

Putting Yourself Into Your Dreams!

This is the time to begin to see yourself as more than you have ever perceived yourself to be. As more capable, more intelligent, and stronger than you have ever seen yourself. Now is the time for you to expand your parameters, to take off the blinders, and to actually place yourself in the position where it is possible for you to do all that you have longed to do.

As you begin to expand your mind, you will get in touch with the positive, more capable aspects of yourself. You will become open to the good that is within you.

Freeing Yourself One Step at a Time!

It's important to emphasize that freedom is a process. You cannot expect to visualize yourself as the captain of a ship if you don't even know port from starboard. The exercises at the end of this chapter are designed to cultivate a consciousness of freedom one step at a time. I encourage you to approach this process in a practical way, so that you don't set yourself up for failure. This is not the time to be impatient. You need to realize that, step by step, moment by moment, day by day...

> *THIS SEVEN-STEP CREATIVE PROCESS*
> *IS GOING TO TAKE YOU*
> *FROM WHERE YOU ARE,*
> *TO WHERE YOU WANT TO BE!*

Freedom Is A State of Mind!

I'm going to ask you to do one new thing a week, just to show yourself that you can. It doesn't have to be anything as monumental as skydiving or running for office. It can be going to a movie by yourself, or enrolling in an exercise class, or baking a cake for a friend, or trying a new hair style, or ordering a new dish at a restaurant, or just about anything that is new, or different from your normal habit.

The goal is to help you understand that freedom is a state of mind. Each of us has the ability to step out of our rut and try new things. By doing this, we understand that we are capable of much more than we previously had believed.

There is something therapeutic about knowing our capabilities, and stretching ourselves every chance we get, that brings about a maturity and poise. These are the very ingredients we need, to work the creative process successfully.

JUST BECAUSE WE HAVEN'T REALIZED OUR POTENTIAL, DOESN'T MEAN IT'S NOT THERE!

It just means that we haven't yet opened our minds to accepting our possibilities and making them work for us.

The tools in this book can help you learn how to release the negative beliefs you currently hold about who you are and what you can accomplish. They can teach you how to recognize and explore the various opportunities for creative fulfillment that are available to you. However, only you can make the decision to step out of your self-imposed prison.

ONLY YOU CAN FREE YOURSELF TO BE YOURSELF.

You will do this only when it becomes necessary to you. When you become worth the risk!

STEP ONE – FREE YOURSELF
KEY IDEAS

- OUR INNERMOST DREAMS REPRESENT THE CREATIVE URGE WITHIN US, SEEKING EXPRESSION.

- IF WE TRULY WANT TO EXPERIENCE FULFILLMENT, WE MUST LISTEN TO THE DESIRES OF OUR HEART, LEARN TO UNDERSTAND THEM, AND TAKE THEM SERIOUSLY.

- LIFE IS A SERIES OF CHOICES. EITHER WE REMAIN LOCKED IN THE SELF-IMPOSED PRISON OF LIMITATION, OR WE FREE OURSELVES TO DISCOVER OUR OPTIONS.

- WE BEGIN TO FREE OURSELVES BY REALIZING THAT WE ARE GREATER THAN WE PRESENTLY BELIEVE OURSELVES TO BE.

- IT IS NOT NECESSARY TO *CHANGE* OURSELVES, BUT TO *BECOME* OURSELVES.

- WE BECOME FREE OF MENTAL AND EMOTIONAL BONDAGE "ONE THOUGHT AT A TIME."

- OUR POTENTIAL FOR HAPPINESS AND SUCCESS IS ALWAYS WITHIN US. NOTHING IS TOO GOOD TO BE TRUE!

EXERCISES TO FREE YOURSELF

> ***"The true value of a human being is judged only by the extent that he is freed of himself."***
>
> ALBERT EINSTEIN

Begin To Take Charge!

Most of us are not really making active choices about how we live our lives. We live, mostly, out of habit. We do the things we are obligated to do ... the things we are expected to do ... and, not necessarily, the things we *want* to do. We have forgotten that we can make choices about how we spend, if not *all* of our time, at least *some* of it. Making choices is empowering. It gives us the freedom of control over our own lives.

LIST 20 THINGS YOU ENJOY DOING.

1. ____________	11. ____________
2. ____________	12. ____________
3. ____________	13. ____________
4. ____________	14. ____________
5. ____________	15. ____________
6. ____________	16. ____________
7. ____________	17. ____________
8. ____________	18. ____________
9. ____________	19. ____________
10. ____________	20. ____________

Now, look at your list and draw a line through the things you do as often as you like. You now are left with a number of things you like to do, but that you either are not doing at all, or not as often as you'd like.

Choose one item from the list that you would LIKE to do, or that you would like to do MORE OFTEN, and designate a time to do it this week. Write this activity in the space provided on the following Freedom Contract. (Make copies of this blank contract, because you will need one for every item on your list that is not marked off. You might not be able to do everything on your list right now, but there's no time limit. Do the things you can, and look for ways to do the rest.)

Do at least one thing from your list each week. Keep referring to your list and adding to it. The idea is to focus on what you *enjoy.* In doing so, you'll find that you are making positive decisions for yourself, because you are worth it. Taking charge of your life will give you a more positive sense of self-worth, and you will begin to feel more deserving of the good things in life.

FREEDOM CONTRACT

Week of /________/________(date)

I, ____ ,
YOUR NAME

AGREE TO FREE MYSELF THIS WEEK, BY MAKING TIME TO ENJOY ____________________

____

____

I WILL NOT FEEL GUILTY FOR DOING THIS. I WILL NOT NEGLECT MY RESPONSIBILITIES IN ORDER TO DO IT. I WILL BEGIN TO REALIZE THAT MY LIFE BELONGS TO ME, AND I HAVE THE FREEDOM TO ENJOY IT.

____
Your Signature

> ***"I want to get you excited about who you are, what you are, what you have, and what can still be for you. I want to inspire you to see that you can go far beyond where you are right now."***
>
> VIRGINIA SATIR

You Have To Say It To Believe It!

We are always making choices, whether we realize it or not. Choosing to speak affirmations frees us from negative thinking and self-imposed limitations.

Affirmations say "yes" to all the good that life has to offer. Affirmations are like a magnet, helping us to become conscious of our inner power, and bringing that power into our experience.

Keep the following affirmations by your bedside. Set aside a few moments as you begin and end each day, and say these affirmations aloud. You will soon feel a greater sense of poise and self-esteem.

I AM STRONGER THAN I THINK I AM.

I AM SMARTER THAN I THINK I AM.

I AM MORE CREATIVE THAN I THINK I AM.

I AM MORE TALENTED THAN I THINK I AM.

I AM MORE INTERESTING THAN I THINK I AM.

I AM MORE CAPABLE THAN I THINK I AM.

I AM MORE LOVABLE THAN I THINK I AM.

Morning Talk

It is extremely important to set a positive tone for the day. Upon awakening each morning, before you get out of bed, affirm the following statement three times:

TODAY I AM FREE.
I CHOOSE TO MAKE THIS A GOOD DAY!

Be Your Own Best Friend!

Think of someone who loves and respects you very much. Perhaps it's your best friend or a favorite relative. This person can be anyone you have ever known, past or present, but it must be someone who truly loves you. How would this person describe you? What would they name as your three greatest strengths? What would they say you needed to improve upon? What would they say about your talents and abilities ... your personality ... your appearance? Write this person's description of you in the space provided.

THIS IS HOW ____________________ WOULD DESCRIBE ME:

____________________ is ____________________
YOUR NAME

____

____

____

____

____

____

____

____

____

____

Is this description different from the way you would describe yourself? How is it different? The description above is from one who loves you. How can you begin to see yourself through the eyes of love? Without a healthy self-image, we can never feel deserving of the best that life has to offer us. Learn to be kind to yourself.

> ***"Self-image sets the boundaries of individual accomplishment."***
>
> MAXWELL MALTZ

The Golden Door Relaxation and Meditation

If you have the cassette that accompanies this book, you can use The Golden Door Meditation on the tape. If not, read this meditation into a tape recorder, with relaxing music in the background, or have someone do it for you. Listen to it at least once a day for one month, and as often as you like, thereafter. This meditation will help you learn to focus on what you want, and believe that you are deserving of it.

Find yourself a comfortable chair in a quiet room. Make certain you are not bothered by tight clothing, and that there are no disturbances likely to occur. Put the pets in another part of the house and unplug your telephone.

Become comfortable in your chair. Begin to relax by taking a big, deep breath, holding it for a second, and exhaling fully and completely, letting go of tension and stress. Continue breathing deeply and evenly.

Now, begin at the top of your head, feel the presence of a warm, relaxing, shimmering, golden light, gently circling your head and moving downward, filling and surrounding the area of your face. Feel your facial muscles relax. Notice how much easier it is to relax your face when you release the tension in your forehead and jaw. Continue to breathe deeply, and affirm, "My face and head are now relaxed. I am comfortable and at peace."

Feel the golden light, warm and radiant, in the area of your neck and shoulders. Take a deep breath, and as you exhale, feel the release of tension, as you affirm, "My neck and shoulders are now relaxed. I am comfortable and at peace."

The gentle light moves easily down your back, enfolding and encircling every muscle. You affirm, "My back muscles are now relaxed. I am comfortable and at peace."

Continuing to breathe deeply, feel the healing light move down your arms. Feel your hands unclenching and relaxing as you affirm, "My arms and hands are now relaxed. I am comfortable and at peace."

Feel the golden, radiant light move farther down your body. Release the tension in your stomach muscles, your thigh muscles, your knees, and your calf muscles as you affirm, "My body is now completely relaxed, I am comfortable and at peace."

Continue to inhale the rich, vibrant air and exhale all of your tension and stress. Begin to feel a heaviness, a calmness throughout every muscle in your body. Your mind is clear and focused, and every time you inhale and exhale, it becomes easier and easier to sense the clarity and brightness of your mind.

Repeat to yourself, "My heartbeat is calm and regular. My breathing is deep and even. My muscles are relaxed and I am at peace."

The golden, shimmering light flows around and through your entire body. Feel its comfort and warmth. Enjoy your body feeling relaxed and free. Enjoy your mind feeling alert and awake and alive.

Begin now to visualize a soft white mist in front of you. As you look into this soothing, swirling haze, you see a form coming toward you, and you feel a sense of thrilling expectation, because you know that this encounter will be the most important one of your life. As the form emerges into the light, you see a person wearing a beautiful, long, flowing, snow-white robe. The robe is billowing in the breeze and it looks as if it must be the softest, most luxurious fabric ever created. As you look closely at this person, you see the face of one totally at peace. It is the most beautiful face you have ever seen. You see all the love and wisdom of the ages reflected on this beautiful face.

You feel so safe... so loved... so cherished and honored. You know, in your heart, that this is the most important person in your life. This is the special friend you have longed for. Your new friend reaches out with both hands and, in a voice so warm and soothing, says, "I am your higher self. I am that part of you that knows no limitation... no fear... no anger... only love and peace. I see you as you really are — wonderful, wise, and strong; deserving of everything good in life. I am with you always. I am inside of you... guiding you... protecting you. I want you to come with me now. I have a very special gift for you."

You reach out both your hands, put them into the hands of your higher self, and stand up. You gaze into that loving face for a moment and then you both walk into the soft, swirling, gentle mist. As you emerge from the other side of the hazy mist, you find yourself at the beginning of a long, white corridor. Notice how trusting you feel, as you willingly walk down the corridor, knowing that you are going to a place that is special and wonderful.

As you come to the end of the corridor, you see an enormous door. It is pure gold, and decorated with precious stones. Your higher self looks at you with eyes of love and complete acceptance, and says, "Enter the golden door. Sit in the quiet of this rich and glorious room, and allow it to shower you with unlimited goodness and beauty. This is the place where your dreams become reality."

The golden door opens, and you walk through it. Inside, is the most spectacular room you have ever seen, beautifully decorated. You see a comfortable-looking chair in the center of the room and walk toward it. You sit in this wonderful chair, and feel your body relax into its contours. Now take a deep breath and exhale. With your eyes closed, feel yourself lifted to the realm of all possibilities. Here is where you can see and feel yourself experiencing your heart's desire. Whatever you can imagine that will make you feel joyous and fulfilled, see it now, feel it with every fiber of your being — become what you desire — experience your happiness. (*Let the music play under the visualization for a few minutes.*)

After a time, you feel a presence, as your higher self enters the room, smiles that warm, loving smile, reaches for your hand, and tells you that it's time to go for today. As you walk back through the golden door into the long, white corridor, you turn around to see the beautiful, golden door slowly close. You now realize that this is your *door and* your *room, always here for you. It is closed, but never locked, and any time you wish, you can come to this place, walk through the golden door into this special room, experience all your dreams coming true... and feel again, how precious and wonderful you are.*

As you return down the white corridor, you feel a deep sense of peace and well-being. You feel your life has a purpose and you are safe and secure.

As you find yourself seated back in your position of meditation, your higher self leans over and embraces you... and promises that whenever you wish, you will meet again to relax, and visit your special room, through the golden door... and experience your dreams coming true.

Your higher self begins to fade from your sight and you hear these words, "Remember that I am with you always. I am the highest part of you. I am your purity... your excellence... your wholeness. Hold on to your dreams. You deserve them... they are yours."

As the mist slowly fades from your vision, you begin to become aware of your surroundings. You feel the chair supporting you. You become conscious of this time and this place. You become aware of a feeling of joy and gratitude, and although you feel very relaxed, you also feel energized and revitalized. You look forward to experiencing the rest of your day. And you know that your higher self is very much with you.. inside of you... guiding you... reminding you that you are so much more than you ever believed yourself to be. And that NOTHING IS TOO GOOD TO BE TRUE, *FOR YOU!*

> ***"Our first awakening reveals that our mind, conditioned as it is to superstition and tradition, is the prison-house in which we dwell."***
>
> JOEL GOLDSMITH

Learn To Recognize Your Automatic Pilot

Beginning tomorrow morning, pay very close attention to everything you do, when you awaken. Try to notice the things you do by rote ... the things you always do the same way, without thinking about them.

Do you always put your shirt on before your pants or skirt? Do you put your left sock on before your right sock, or vice-versa? Do you take the same route to work every day? Do you always listen to the same radio station in your car? Is everything always arranged the same way on your desk, or work place?

For the next few days, choose one thing a day, and do it differently from the way you normally do it. Put on the other sock first. Hold the telephone in your other hand. Take a different route to work. If you typically eat in front of the TV, eat in the dining room. If you normally eat in the dining room, take a tray to the patio or living room. It doesn't matter what you choose to do differently, just as long as it is something that you nearly always do the same way.

This exercise is designed to make you more aware of yourself and the world around you; to open your mind to the fact that we are all creatures of habit, and that we have choices and opportunities we are not exercising.

Do You Know What You're Doing?

Another good focusing exercise is to set aside some time each day to observe yourself in action. Try narrating your activities, in the third person, as they happen." (Your name) is getting out of bed. ... is walking down the hall to the kitchen. ... is opening the refrigerator door. ... is taking the juice out of the refrigerator, etc." You'll be surprised for how short a period you can keep this up ... a few minutes at the most.

The point of both of these exercises is to illustrate that most of us are walking around virtually asleep, much of the time. We forfeit many of our choices by not being conscious of them. This is how life slips up on us. We turn around one day, find ourselves in a situation we never planned, and wonder how we got there.

We can free ourselves from much of our "automatic living" by simply paying attention to our lives. There will be more about the art of self-observation in Step Two.

Be sure you spend all the time you need on these Step One Exercises. The idea is for you to feel worthy and deserving of your good before you go on to those in Step Two.

Freeing yourself is the crucial first step in the creative process. Until you can release the limiting beliefs you currently hold, about who you are and the capabilities you possess, you cannot hope to recognize and explore the various opportunities for creative fulfillment that are open to you.

AFFIRMATION

I RELEASE ALL LIMITING BELIEFS. I AM FREE TO EXPRESS THE HIGHEST WITHIN ME.

RECOMMENDED READING

GETTING UNSTUCK, Breaking Through Your Barriers To Change. Dr. Sidney B. Simon. 1988. Warner Books

Techniques for breaking down your resistance to change, and freeing yourself from limited and unsatisfactory values.

ONE PERSON CAN MAKE A DIFFERENCE, Gerald G. Jampolsky, M.D. 1990. Bantam Books, New York

A collection of interviews with unforgettable people who are making use of their unlimited potential. Inspiring examples of the effectiveness that can be achieved by each of us.

PATHFINDERS, Gail Sheehy. 1982. Bantam Books, New York

An inspiring and informative account of individuals, from all walks of life, who have freed themselves by meeting and overcoming challenges—both personal and professional.

PSYCHO CYBERNETICS, Maxwell Maltz. 1960. Pocket Books, New York

Your self-image affects virtually everything you do. This classic text, dealing with self-image psychology and creative visualization, is as relevant today as when it was introduced over 30 years ago.

TRAVELLING FREE, How To Recover From The Past By Changing Your Beliefs. Mandy Evans. 1991. Yes You Can Press, Encinitas, California

This book is compatible with 12-Step Anonymous Programs, but is not limited to those in recovery.

STEP TWO

KNOW YOURSELF

The secret
of getting
what you want
is knowing
who you are!

***"What lies
behind us
and what lies
before us
are tiny matters
compared to
what lies
within us."***

RALPH WALDO EMERSON

I always wanted to play the piano. I wanted not only to be able to read music, but also to have the ability to improvise and embellish musical arrangements to fit my own personal style. I didn't just want to play the piano ... I wanted to play *exceptionally well.*

I took enough piano lessons to realize, however, that I didn't have the same natural ability in that area that I had in singing, for example. So while I really would have enjoyed having skill at the piano, I knew that if I wanted to become accomplished, I was going to have to work twice as hard as someone with natural ability. I wasn't willing to do that. I wanted to play the piano — but not enough to practice!

Looking back, I can see how this insight saved me a lot of frustration and allowed me to focus on the areas in which I had a greater opportunity for success.

Self-knowledge is the second step in the creative process. Once you have begun to free yourself from your negative and outworn beliefs, it is imperative that you begin to understand exactly who you are, and what you are willing and able to do.

Generally speaking, we are capable of doing a number of things well, but doing something well doesn't necessarily bring us happiness. If we want to experience the joy of true fulfillment, we must look within ourselves to get in touch with the deepest desires of our heart.

Self-knowledge will help you discover what kind of temperament you have, what your strengths are, and whether or not the interests you have are compatible with the skills you possess, or are willing to cultivate.

I'm not saying that you should avoid everything that doesn't come easily to you. I'm convinced that if my longing to play the piano had been a "burning desire," I would have worked as hard as I needed, to come up with the necessary skills. I probably would not have become as great a pianist as somebody with a natural talent, who had worked equally as hard, but I would have learned to play well enough to feel as though I had achieved my goal.

What You Don't Know Can Hurt You!

The mind is virtually unlimited in its capacity to assimilate and retain information. Most of what we learn during our lives goes into the subconscious phase of our mind ... and stays there! The subconscious is the vast storehouse of all that we ever have learned, and of every feeling that has had an impact on our lives. We are able to draw some of this information forth when we need it, but often we are not conscious of possessing this knowledge, because we experience only a small percentage of our mind power.

Some feelings are suppressed in our subconscious because, for one reason or another, we believe we are unable to cope with them. We might not remember the events that caused the feelings, but the feelings are there — not "healed," just suppressed. Sometimes an event will occur that is similar to one that caused us to suppress a memory. Often, when this happens, an automatic response is triggered and those stored feelings come to the surface. We find ourselves reacting automatically, in much the same way as we did when the original event took place. This type of response is often referred to as "having our buttons pushed."

When this occurs, we're frequently accused of over-reacting. Our responses can be very confusing to ourselves and those around us, because we're actually responding, not to current situations, but to events that might have happened to us years ago. This type of subconscious response can create self-defeating habit patterns. These patterns can interfere with the successful accomplishment of our goals and the attainment of our dreams.

What Don't You Remember?

In one of my workshops, called "Secrets of Self-Knowledge," an example of a self-defeating habit pattern was shared by a student.

Joan is a woman in her mid-forties. She works for the federal government in a data processing department. Part of Joan's job is making presentations, and instructing her co-workers in new program designs. She presents herself as a very capable and articulate professional today, but, according to Joan, this was not always the case. She told us her story:

"When I was about nine years old, I was asked to make a short announcement at a school assembly. I was very nervous, but I did the best I could, and thought I'd done pretty well.

"After school, my older brother, who had been present at the assembly, came up to me and said,

'That was a dumb speech. You're always saying something stupid!' I could feel the heat rush to my face as he and his friends laughed at me.

"I was mortified! I was devastated! The encounter with my brother was so painful that I suppressed the memory of it for many years, but it affected my communication skills from that time forward. I was afraid that no one would be interested in anything I had to say. If I was asked to speak in front of people, I would literally lose my voice. I was terrified that I would embarrass myself by saying something that didn't make sense.

"My frustration at not being able to express myself was enormous. Every time I had to communicate verbally, I would freeze up. I'm not just talking about speaking in front of an audience, either — that, of course, was simply out of the question — but I couldn't even respond to my boss without stuttering and stammering.

"Many years later, I was working in the data processing division of a large company. I had been passed over for promotion time after time, even though I had more seniority than anyone else in my department.

"Then one day the job of assistant division manager became available. I was one of four people being considered for the position. They had to go through the motions of considering me because of my seniority, but I knew that I would never get the promotion. The job would require written and verbal reports to upper management, and presentations to other divisions. I just didn't see how I could ever hope to function effectively in that type of job, even if I could pull off the interview.

"My self-esteem was at an all-time low. Not because I felt incapable, but because I knew that I was extremely capable, in every way but one. I had all the knowledge and experience I needed for the job, but I just couldn't make myself understood verbally. My fears were holding me back from something that I wanted very much, but I simply didn't know how to overcome them.

"I began to do some real soul-searching. I took stock of my life up to that point. I looked at all the opportunities I had missed because of fear. I wanted this new job so much, but I knew that I would have to do something to stop this pattern of self-defeat. If I was ever going to progress professionally or experience any real peace in my life, I had to take some action.

"I made the decision to enroll in a Dale Carnegie course. I also entered counseling and began to keep a journal. In this journal, I wrote down my feelings and reactions to practically everything that happened to me. I tried to determine which of my beliefs and attitudes was the basis for these reactions. During my counseling sessions, we uncovered the event from my past, in which my brother made the devastating remark about my speech. I began to get a really clear picture of where some of my responses were coming from.

"I wish I could say that I got the job and everything was happy ever after, but that's not what happened. The job went to someone else. However, the work I did, in preparation for the possibility of getting that job, changed my life. I was finally able to see myself in a more realistic light. As I gathered more and more evidence that what I had to say held interest for people, my fear began to slip away.

"A year or so after this happened, I applied for the job I have now, and got it. I never would have had the courage, even to apply for the job, before I did this work on myself.

"I now know that I spent over 20 years of my life with a totally distorted image of myself. And all because of a remark made, most likely, out of sibling rivalry."

No matter how intelligent and sophisticated we might be, it seems we are often slaves to our emotional subconscious responses. Unfortunately, for most of us, we seldom make the connection between the past and the present without a good deal of contemplation and introspection.

Joan overcame a difficult emotional problem through dedication and a lot of hard work. She wanted it enough to be willing to devote a considerable amount of time to self-discovery, and through this effort she gained the self-confidence she needed to make the necessary changes in her life.

Breaking the Bondage of Fear and Frustration!

Joan's lack of self-knowledge caused her to misunderstand herself and those around her. What she had always considered a character defect, her inability to verbally interact with others, could, in fact, be attributed to a specific event — a memory she had suppressed for years. Acquiring self-knowledge allowed Joan to recognize and release her fear.

To become conscious of the power our subconscious mind has over our actions and reactions puts us in a very powerful position. It reminds us of the choices we can make. It helps us to understand that, while we might have fears and hurt feelings, we cannot continue to allow them to affect our present experiences. We can let the past BE the past!

Discover Your Hidden Power

It's important to realize that our subconscious mind, in addition to being a storehouse of information, is the reservoir of the tremendous power and potential inherent within us. Once we release our negative and self-defeating habit patterns, we become free to express our positive and powerful nature.

> *AS WE CLEAR THE WAY*
> *OUR "IMPRISONED SPLENDOR"*
> *COMES SHINING THROUGH.*

Whose Idea Was This, Anyway?

A lack of self-knowledge about what we like or enjoy, sometimes causes us to confuse our likes with what other people want us to do. Do you often find yourself asking why you made a particular choice? Actually, in many cases, we didn't choose it because it was what we wanted, but because it was expected of us by our spouse, our parent, our boss, etc. Of course, there is nothing inherently wrong with deciding to do what other people want us to do... as long as we know that's why we're doing it.

Self-knowledge also makes us aware of our talents and abilities. We often spend a lot of time attempting to cultivate abilities that we don't really have or that are not natural to us. The result is that we are never as successful and fulfilled as we can be.

Who is making your decisions?

> *BECAUSE WE DON'T REALIZE OUR TRUE POTENTIAL,*
> *WE'RE OFTEN AIMING TOO LOW*
> *... OR IN THE WRONG DIRECTION!*

Which One of You is Reading This Book?

As we begin to study ourselves, we learn to recognize all of the different parts of our personality that make up the whole of us. These different facets of our nature, our "subpersonalities" as they have been called, exist inside of us as parent, child, spouse, student, employer, and all of the other roles we play in life. We need to be aware of which of our selves is responding and reacting to people and situations.

Books such as GAMES PEOPLE PLAY by Eric Berne, and I'M OK, YOU'RE OK by Thomas Harris, have introduced the concept of the threefold personality, "Parent," "Child." and "Adult." Others, such as YOUR INNER CHILD OF THE PAST by W. Hugh Missildine, help us understand ourselves as multifaceted beings, capable of all kinds of inner conflict.

For example, we say things like, "Part of me wants to do it and part of me doesn't," or "I can't imagine what made me say that." Many of us find ourselves paying off obligations to which another of our selves has committed us. "How did I get myself into this," asks one part of self to another.

THE KNOWLEDGE THAT WE ARE MANY SELVES IS IMPERATIVE TO SUCCESSFUL SELF-OBSERVATION.

It's very important to understand that the feelings or responses of any one of our many selves is never representative of the whole of us. Some of our selves are fearful, and these tend to present themselves at any important crossroad in our life. As soon as we become aware that these apprehensions are present in only a part of our personality, we can more objectively weigh the pros and cons of any major decision.

> **Wizard of Oz to Cowardly Lion:**
> ***"There is no living thing***
> ***that is not afraid when it faces danger.***
> ***True courage is in facing danger***
> ***when you ARE afraid."***
>
> FRANK L. BAUM

Why You Do The Things You Do!

There can be no self-knowledge without self-observation. Self-observation is one of our greatest tools. It is the ability to step aside from our involvement in a current situation, and evaluate it from an objective perspective. It is the ability to watch ourselves at any given time and ask, "What is happening here? What am I feeling? What am I thinking? How does my behavior appear to others? Which of my selves is reacting to this situation?" It's important that we cultivate the "observing self" within us so that we can objectively evaluate our responses.

We must be careful not to confuse *self-observation* with *self-condemnation!* Our goal is not to *blame* ourselves, but to *understand* ourselves. Through self-observation we are able to discover habit patterns. We are able to discern when and how those patterns developed. We are able to make rational choices about how to get ourselves out of those patterns.

SELF-OBSERVATION IS THE KEY TO SELF-KNOWLEDGE, AND IT IS SELF-KNOWLEDGE THAT BRINGS ABOUT CHANGE.

Self-knowledge helps us understand why we do the things we do. We need to ask ourselves, periodically, "What are my reasons for doing what I'm doing? Do I really want to do this, or am I doing it because someone else thinks I should do it? Am I doing it only to prove a point or to 'get even'? Do I understand the consequences of what I am doing?"

When we truly know ourselves, we are less susceptible to being manipulated by others. We begin to think more deeply and clearly. We become able to recognize the times when we are being motivated by guilt, revenge, spite, or other reasons that might not be for our highest good.

How To Conquer The Rip Van Winkle Syndrome

Most people are, metaphorically speaking, asleep — entranced automatons controlled by mechanical habits of thought, perception, and behavior.

Much of our suffering is useless — unknowingly created through our misperceptions of the world around us, and our own nature and desires. If we can wake up to a more realistic perception of ourselves and our world, our actions will be more appropriate and effective, and we will live more creative and fulfilling lives.

By working through the exercises at the end of this chapter, you will become able to evaluate yourself more clearly and objectively. You will become more conscious of your habit patterns and behaviors. You will begin to recognize more of your inherent strengths and abilities.

One of the most important things we can gain from this study in self-knowledge is the ability to take responsibility for ourselves and for changing our attitudes and beliefs. Like self-observation, taking responsibility is not the same as focusing blame or condemnation on ourselves. Taking responsibility means recognizing that it is within our power to make changes in our lives that will cause us to be happier, and more creative. It also means being able to learn from past mistakes.

THE LESSONS LEARNED FROM MISTAKES ARE SOME OF THE MOST VALUABLE ONES IN OUR QUEST FOR SELF-KNOWLEDGE!

When I was in ministerial school, I was invited to speak to the congregation of one of the Unity churches in Kansas City. It was my first Sunday talk outside the classroom, and I wanted to do really well. As always, I did a lot of research and made copious notes.

As I left the house on the morning of the talk, I was excited, but not really nervous, because I felt very well prepared. I had everything I needed, in my trusty little blue notebook, to give an inspiring talk.

I arrived at the church a few minutes before the service was to begin, and decided to glance once more at my notes. I opened my notebook and saw — not my carefully prepared lesson — but an assignment sheet from my philosophy of religion class. I DIDN'T HAVE MY NOTES!!! I panicked! Never before had I attempted to give a speech without a full set of notes.

The initial shock subsided after a few minutes, as I began to organize my thoughts and pray for guidance. I sat through the opening of the service, breathing deeply and affirming over and over, "I know what to say, and I say it."

By the time I was introduced, I was calm enough to deliver my lesson. Soon I began to relax and enjoy myself. It wasn't exactly the same talk I had so carefully prepared. In some ways it was better — fresh, alive and spontaneous.

On the drive home, I realized that the experience had been a gift. I now knew that I could speak effectively without being tied to my notes. My mistake taught me a valuable lesson about myself, and I became aware of an ability I didn't know I had.

Every situation can become an opportunity for self-discovery. How little we know of ourselves until we are faced with challenges. But why must we wait for unexpected circumstances to cause us to wake up? It is possible, through study and inner searching, to begin to learn about ourselves right now. There is so much more to all of us than we can imagine. We have talents and abilities we haven't even begun to explore. By discovering them now, we can make use of them, to enrich our lives, and the lives of those around us.

Self-discovery is an exciting expedition. Some of the things you learn about yourself will be things you might not like — but, I guarantee the majority of things you discover will give you the power and the strength that you need to rise above any obstacles on your path.

There's A Hole In My Sidewalk

Autobiography in Five Short Chapters

I walk down the street.
There is a deep hole in the sidewalk.
I fall in.
I am lost ... I am hopeless.
It isn't my fault.
It takes forever to find a way out.

I walk down the same street.
There is a deep hole in the sidewalk.
I pretend I don't see it.
I fall in again.
I can't believe I am in the same place.
But, it isn't my fault.
It still takes a long time to get out.

I walk down the same street.
There is a deep hole in the sidewalk.
I see it is there.
I still fall in ... it's a habit.
My eyes are open
I know where I am.
It is my fault.
I get out immediately.

I walk down the same street.
There is a deep hole in the sidewalk.
I walk around it.

I walk down another street.

PORTIA NELSON

STEP TWO – KNOW YOURSELF
KEY IDEAS

- SELF-KNOWLEDGE ENABLES US TO RECOGNIZE AND DEVELOP OUR TALENTS AND SKILLS.

- SUBCONSCIOUS HABIT PATTERNS CAN CAUSE US TO CONFUSE PAST HURTS WITH PRESENT REALITIES.

- THE MORE WE KNOW ABOUT OURSELVES, THE BETTER ABLE WE ARE TO DISCOVER SELF-DEFEATING HABIT PATTERNS AND RISE ABOVE THEM.

- SELF-KNOWLEDGE HELPS US UNDERSTAND WHY WE DO WHAT WE DO.

- AS WE BECOME AWARE OF THE MANY "SELVES" THAT COMPRISE OUR TOTAL PERSONALITY, WE LEARN TO DEAL MORE EFFECTIVELY WITH INNER CONFLICT.

- SELF-OBSERVATION IS NOT SELF-CONDEMNATION. OUR GOAL IS NOT TO *BLAME* OURSELVES, BUT TO *UNDERSTAND* OURSELVES.

- SOME OF OUR MOST VALUABLE INSIGHTS CAN BE DISCOVERED THROUGH OUR "MISTAKES."

EXERCISES FOR SELF-KNOWLEDGE

> ***"We must come to study***
> ***and know ourselves...***
> ***our motivation ...***
> ***and our exceptional capacity***
> ***to become what we dream***
> ***we can become."***
>
> EDGAR D. MITCHELL

Describe Your Childhood!

There are no "right answers" to this quiz. It is a tool to help you put the pieces together and begin to form a picture of who you are. Use a notebook for this exercise. Take all the space you need to give complete answers.

1. What were you like as a child? What did you enjoy doing? What made it enjoyable? What did you dislike doing? Why?

2. Describe your relationship with your parents. Your siblings.

3. How did you get along in school? What were your favorite subjects? What did you want to be when you grew up?

4. Who was your best friend, and why? Who was your "worst enemy," and why? What did you learn from these relationships.

5. What are your most significant childhood memories? a) the most positive. b) the most negative. What did you learn from those experiences at the time? Have you gained any new insights about those memories in recent years?

6. Can you tie specific impressions from your childhood to behaviors, attitudes, or beliefs about yourself that you express as an adult? Which of these expressions work for you today? Which ones need to be revised?

> ***"True education is the process of waking up to life."***
>
> ERIC BUTTERWORTH

Who Are You Today?

1. Do you tend to enjoy parties, or do you attend mostly out of obligation?

2. Do you usually feel more comfortable working in a group, or on your own?

3. Generally speaking, do you carefully consider all factors before making a decision, or do you often act on the spur of the moment?

4. Do you find that you tend to accomplish tasks more effectively when you have a definite timetable, or when you are allowed to work at your own pace?

5. Do you enjoy interacting with many people at once, or are you more comfortable with one-on-one encounters?

6. When you browse in a bookstore, do you generally gravitate toward fiction or non-fiction?

7. If you were in school now, what would you enjoy studying? Why?

8. What gives you the most satisfaction out of going to school? a) researching and accumulating new information____ b) interacting with other students____ c) getting good grades____.

9. What are your favorite topics of conversation?

10. Name the last good book you read. What did you enjoy about it?

11. Do you enjoy being around children?
very much____ occasionally____ seldom____.

12. Do you enjoy being around animals?
very much____ occasionally____ seldom____.

13. Generally speaking, do you enjoy a) talking more than listening, b) listening more than talking.

14. When a group is making social plans, are you generally content to a) let someone else decide what to do, b) take an active part in the decision-making process?

15. How do you feel about speaking in front of an audience? a) It terrifies me, I'd much rather not

do it; b) It's somewhat scary, but challenging; c) It's fun and stimulating.

16. At around 9:00 PM do you a) think about going to bed; b) feel awake and alert?

17. Do you feel the most energetic a) during the morning hours; b) during the evening hours?

18. Which do you enjoy most? a) making plans; b) carrying plans out.

19. Do you usually a) take things and people at face value; b) analyze and look beyond appearances?

20. When people tell you their problems: a) do you feel burdened and unsure of what to say? b) are you interested and compassionate?

These questions have no right or wrong answers. They are designed strictly for self-knowledge. Look over your answers. What conclusions can you draw about yourself? Have you learned anything you didn't know about yourself?

For an in-depth study of your personality type, I strongly suggest that you read the book PLEASE UNDERSTAND ME, listed at the end of this chapter in Recommended Reading.

> ***"It is possible to tap the good and creative potentials deep within you, so that they emerge and find expression in everything you do."***
>
> NORMAN VINCENT PEALE

Whom Do You Admire?

Think of several people whom you like or respect. List their names, the qualities that attract you, and the ways in which they demonstrate these qualities.

Example:

NAME:	**QUALITIES:**
Susan	*Integrity* (Always says what she believes, even if it's not popular.) *Warmth* (Seems genuinely interested when she asks about you.)
Uncle Bill	*Honesty* (Doesn't try to blame others for his mistakes.) *Optimism* (Looks for the good in every situation.)

NAME:	**QUALITIES:**
________________	______________________________
	______________________________
	______________________________
	______________________________

NAME:	**QUALITIES:**
________________	______________________________
	______________________________
	______________________________
	______________________________

NAME: __________ **QUALITIES:** __________

NAME: __________ **QUALITIES:** __________

NAME: __________ **QUALITIES:** __________

NAME: __________ **QUALITIES:** __________

NAME: __________ **QUALITIES:** __________

It is likely that you admire these qualities because you possess them in one degree or another. Give this some thought. In the following space, write the ways in which you can cultivate these qualities in your own life.

"You feel the way you do right now because of the thoughts you are thinking at this moment."

DAVID D. BURNS

Keep A Journal

Take a few minutes at the end of each day to document some of the events from your day. Record your feelings and responses as accurately as you can. For each entry, ask yourself these questions:

Were my initial responses based on current circumstances, or were they from the past?

Did I make assumptions about other people?

In what other ways could I have responded to this same situation?

Now, write a second account, from the perspective of your "observing self." Does your observer see things differently? What are the differences in the two accounts? Which is more accurate? Remember, just observe ... do not judge yourself harshly.

What Pushes Your Buttons?

1. How often do you feel angry?

____

____

What kinds of things cause you to respond in an angry way? ____________________________________

____

____

How do you express your anger? _______________

____

____

Do you generally hold on to angry feelings, or do you "forgive and forget?" ____________________

____

How do you define forgiveness? ________________

____

2. How often do you get your feelings hurt? For what reasons? ____________________________________

____

____

____

____

Do you usually share your pain, or keep it to yourself? ____________________________________

____

____

____

____

3. What causes you to feel afraid? _____________

____

____

How do you handle your fear? ________________

____

____

____

Your responses to these questions are very important to your understanding of yourself. Can you see areas in which you are reacting to the past instead of the present? Are you still holding on to old hurts? what do these responses tell you about yourself?

Discover Your Talents

1. What is your greatest and most memorable achievement? What made it so special?

2. What type of activity gives you the deepest mental and emotional satisfaction?

3. Imagine yourself receiving an award for your accomplishments. What would be written on your plaque?

4. How often do you feel joyful? What makes you happy? ______________________________

____

____

____

5. Do you believe you deserve to experience happiness and peace of mind? ________________

____

____

6. How can you go about creating more happiness in your life? Be specific! ________________

____

____

____

____

____

____

It is not necessary to complete this questionnaire at one sitting. Give yourself time to contemplate your answers. Remember, the more you understand about yourself, the better able you are to interpret the desires of your heart and decide how best to express them.

AFFIRMATION

I KNOW MYSELF
I ACCEPT MYSELF
I AM TRUE TO MYSELF

RECOMMENDED READING

BORN TO WIN, Muriel James, Ed.D. & Dorothy Jongeward, Ph.D. 1971. Penguin Books, New York

A Transactional Analysis classic. Helpful in understanding our Parent, Adult, and Child personality characteristics.

CREATIVE BREAKTHROUGHS, Tap the Power of your Unconscious Mind, Jill Morris, Ph.D. 1992. Time-Warner, New York

A great help in understanding how our subconscious responses profoundly affect every area of our lives.

HOME COMING, Reclaiming and Championing Your Inner Child, John Bradshaw. 1990. Bantam Books, New York

An informative guide to understanding and overcoming the experiences from our past that affect our responses and behavior in the present.

IF YOU COULD HEAR WHAT I CANNOT SAY, Dr. Nathaniel Brandon. 1985. Bantam Books, New York

Esteemed psychologist Nathaniel Brandon has created an excellent workbook to help us understand, and learn to communicate, our needs and desires.

MAN THE MANIPULATOR, Everett L. Shostrum. 1967. Bantam Books, New York

In this classic book, Dr. Shostrum helps us to identify some of our basic survival skills, and gives us tools for getting what we want through honest and open communication.

PLEASE UNDERSTAND ME, Character & Temperament Types David Keirsey and Marilyn Bates. 1978. Distributed by Prometheus Nemesis Book Co. California

This invaluable study in self-knowledge is based on the Myers-Briggs Type Indicator test. Highly recommended as a first step in learning why you do the things you do, and respond the way you do.

TAMING YOUR GREMLIN, A Guide To Enjoying Yourself, Richard D. Carson. 1983. Harper & Row, New York

A creative and practical approach to identifying and transforming the self-defeating aspects of your personality.

THE BOOK OF QUESTIONS, Gregory Stock, Ph.D.. 1987. Workman Publishers, New York

A challenging and entertaining tool for self-discovery. Can be used alone as a catalyst for self-understanding, or with friends, as a lively and revealing group activity.

YOUR MANY FACES, The First Step To Being Loved, Virginia Satir. 1978. Celestial Arts, California

An introduction to our multi-faceted personality. Helps us learn to accept and appreciate our many selves.

STEP THREE

DEDICATE YOURSELF

Dedicate:
To commit to a specific idea...
to channel your energies
in a single direction,
despite all obstacles,
until that idea
becomes a reality!

"... if you do follow your bliss,
you put yourself on a kind of track
that has been there all the while,
waiting for you,
and the life that you
ought to be living
is the one you are living.
When you can see that,
you begin to meet people
who are in the field of your bliss,
and they open the doors for you.
I say, follow your bliss
and don't be afraid,
and doors will open
where you didn't know
they were going to be."

JOSEPH CAMPBELL

Once we know what our interests and deep desires are, it is time to set some goals, and dedicate ourselves to expressing them in our lives. In fact, we might even feel *compelled* to express them if we want to have peace of mind.

We experience a tremendous sense of well-being when we're in our right niche — when we're doing what we love to do and what we are meant to do. We also find a sense of joy and enthusiasm that allows us to embrace life in a rich and rewarding way.

If You Want To Enough!

"Nothing in the world can take the place of persistence. Talent will not; nothing is more common than unsuccessful men with talent. Genius will not; unrewarded genius is almost a proverb. Education will not; the world is full of educated derelicts. Persistence and determination alone are omnipotent."

CALVIN COOLIDGE

These are very important words. An understanding of the need for persistence and determination can mean the difference between fulfillment and frustration.

As you pursue your dream, it's inevitable that you will suffer some disappointments along the way. I urge you to honor and acknowledge your feelings of defeat when they occur, and make every effort to find people who will support and encourage you during these dark periods.

Try not to judge your experiences as "failures". An apparent failure can serve as an opportunity to develop strength and maturity — qualities that will be an enormous help to you in reaching your goals.

JUST BECAUSE WE FIND IT NECESSARY TO TAKE A DIFFERENT PATH, DOESN'T MEAN THAT WE WON'T ARRIVE AT OUR DESTINATION.

Overcoming the Obstacles on the Path!

With deep dedication and sufficient self-knowledge, you are not as likely to misinterpret obstacles as signs that you should give up your goal. In our culture, we too often believe that if a goal is worthwhile, if it is "meant to succeed," it should follow along a smooth path with no deterrents. We are quick to label apparent obstacles as "omens" or "signs" that mean we should turn back or abandon our goal.

This belief can be very counter-productive. When we make a commitment, we are agreeing to follow through on a goal until it is accomplished, even though part of the process may be difficult and frustrating for us. We must believe in ourselves strongly enough to realize that the outcome is going to be worth the struggle.

I wish I could tell you there is a way to achieve your goals without a great deal of effort and without disappointments along the way. Challenges will arise, but be careful not to assign the wrong meaning to them. I don't believe that a setback, in and of itself, is a deterrent or a "sign" that the universe is trying to "tell us something." That is pure superstition, and has no place in this creative process. A great deal of knowledge can be obtained by overcoming obstacles, and as we experience these triumphs, we are able to get in touch with an inner strength and fortitude that can only bolster our resolve to reach our goal.

WHEN WE COMMIT OURSELVES TOTALLY TO AN IDEAL, WE WILL FIND THAT WE HAVE A LOT MORE STRENGTH AND SUPPORT THAN WE EVER DREAMED POSSIBLE.

Many people are not aware of the kind of dedication and perseverance that the human spirit possesses. We are capable of extraordinary determination and achievement when we are truly dedicated to an idea. This exceptional drive usually manifests when it appears that we have come up against insurmountable obstacles.

WHEN ALL ELSE FAILS ... GO WITHIN!

Runners are familiar with the experience of reaching a point in the run where it seems as if they simply can't go on. Their legs are turning to rubber. Their lungs are about to burst. But, if they are determined, they will continue to push themselves. Finally, their endorphins will kick in, and give them a surge of strength, and the remainder of the run becomes quite pleasurable. In other words, something within them comes forth to carry them farther than they believed they could go.

We, too, have a dedication and a force inside us — one that we might not know we have — and we, too, can surpass our own expectations and achieve much greater goals than we ever expected. It takes a tremendous amount of dedication — but, we all know that if our desire is strong enough we'll find a way. It also takes faith, not only in our ability to accomplish our goal, but faith in the power of our God-given potential.

The "Hero" Within Us All!

Overcoming obstacles and the process that we go through in order to achieve our goals, is beautifully characterized by author and scholar, Joseph Campbell, in his popular book, HERO WITH A THOUSAND FACES. Campbell reveals the potential for greatness within each of us as he tells of the "hero's journey." This hero's journey is an archetype of human growth and development. It is about humankind's quest for truth.

The hero's journey begins with an individual who is searching for meaning and purpose, and who leaves familiar and comfortable surroundings to venture into unknown territory. Along the way, the individual encounters great difficulties and what appear to be insurmountable obstacles. In overcoming these obstacles, the hero experiences a great victory and a profound sense of inner peace.

Anytime we set out to explore new ideas or to conquer new worlds, there is no doubt we are going to meet up with some very strange and very different kinds of experiences, some that might threaten to overwhelm us. This does not mean, however, that for these reasons alone, we need to abandon our search. The "hero" continues moving forward and, not only achieves the goal, but realizes some knowledge, at a very deep level, that could not have been anticipated when the journey began.

YOU ARE THE HERO OF YOUR OWN LIFE!

Through this example of the hero's journey, we see that obstacles, rather than being signs or clues that we have made a wrong choice and should turn away from our goal, can often be understood to be an important part of that goal — the part that ultimately carries the greatest significance and the greatest value.

In an age of instant everything — when a lot of what we want and need is pretty much handed to us — it is sometimes difficult to realize just how necessary the overcoming spirit is to any creative endeavor.

Consider the oyster. Occasionally, a tiny grain of sand works its way into the oyster's shell. The sand is a great irritation to the oyster, and to overcome its discomfort, the oyster coats the sand with layers of aragonite crystals known as nacre. After a period of time, this nacre coating forms a small, round object ... we call it a pearl! So you see, in overcoming its irritation, the oyster creates a thing of great beauty and value.

By following this seven-step creative process, you will discover the place within you that can take you far beyond your current understanding of how strong you are. Your strength will sustain you through unforeseen circumstances that you think, right now, are more than you can handle. You do have what it takes, and it is this realization that is the most important part of commitment.

YOU HAVE WHAT IT TAKES
IN ORDER TO DO
WHAT YOU NEED TO DO!

You have made a true commitment when you are so dedicated to an idea that you are willing to explore the dimensions of your own mind and heart, to find a strength you didn't know you had. A strength that will sustain you as your dream becomes a reality.

Why You Should Keep Your Dream Open-Ended!

It's important to recognize exactly what it is about a goal that is attracting you. You should explore other avenues of achieving that goal before you decide there is only one way you can be happy. In order to begin your commitment, it's best not to start with wanting a "thing," but with being committed simply to using your talents that are aching to be expressed. So, the first stage in making a commitment is a broad one.

COMMIT TO THE FULFILLMENT OF AN IDEA RATHER THAN A SPECIFIC GOAL.

If we believe there is only one way for us to experience our dreams we leave ourselves open to a great deal of stress and frustration. For years, I believed that a life in the theater was the only way I could express my talents. I didn't realize that my talents, or the talents of any of us, can be expressed in a number of ways.

It is far better to dedicate ourselves to sharing our talents, than it is to expressing in a specific line of work. A lot of things can happen. We can have accidents. We can lose our abilities to perform in a certain way. Technological advancements can wipe out the need for our particular service. This is why so many rehabilitation centers are concerned with "redirecting" a person's talents. Just because a certain thing becomes unavailable to us doesn't mean life is over. Our talents and skills can be used in a variety of ways.

WE EXPERIENCE FULFILLMENT, NOT FROM DOING A PARTICULAR THING, BUT BY EXPRESSING WHO WE ARE.

A rose is not complete because it grows in a particular setting. It will still experience its essence, its fragrance, and its beauty whether it grows in a nursery, your backyard, or in the White House rose garden.

I'm often asked how I got from a career in entertaining to a career in the ministry. These two things seem worlds apart, and in some ways they are. In some ways, however, it's easy to see how the same talents and skills can be used in both professions. The desire to express verbally, the empathy, compassion and understanding of human nature, the desire to reach a large number of people, and the wish to contribute to the well-being of others, are evident in both lines of work.

If I had realized that what I had inside of me to give was something that could be shared in more ways than one, I would have felt far less frustrated and powerless during the days when I was unhappy with my career in the theater. I think it is possible to get our fill of a certain line of work without thinking we have to give up our talents when we give up the job.

I'm not suggesting that we don't need to be persistent in the pursuit of a specific goal. Focusing our energies on specifics is important and necessary to the manifestation process. But the ultimate dedication — the kind I understand today, and the kind I'm recommending to you — takes place on a deeper level. It's the dedication to expressing particular *talents* and *qualities* — without becoming too dependent on the circumstances surrounding the expression.

Once you realize that what you have to give is greater than a specific line of work, then no matter who goes out of business, or what happens to alter or change your plans, you know you can never be thwarted in your self-expression. Circumstances can change, but your success does not depend on any one particular thing. It comes from expressing the essence of who you are, and there are many ways to do that.

How to Research Your Dream!

There is more than one way to achieve a result. If the goal is one of expressing yourself through visual arts, for example, you might want to investigate the fields of commercial art, photography, architecture, film, fashion, jewelry or furniture design, landscaping, cosmetology, flower-arranging, etc.

Perhaps you are at your best when you are interacting with other people. You might want to consider one of the helping professions such as medicine, the ministry, counseling, teaching, customer service etc. There are many, many different methods you can use to express yourself in a meaningful way. The point is to leave your options open, within a certain range, until you have researched the activity and have an understanding of what you are getting yourself into. Then you can continue to work with your dedication to that one idea until it becomes more specific… until that desire to write becomes a desire to write about a certain thing … until the desire to help people becomes a desire to enter a particular branch of medicine or social work.

Brainstorming Your Options

Brainstorming is the process of writing down, without evaluating, all possibilities that might be a way of fulfilling yourself creatively. No idea is too outlandish during the brainstorming process. Put all of them on your list. Once you have a broad spectrum of possibilities, you can narrow them down into a list of probabilities or viable options for you.

Remember, the only commitment you have made at this point is to expressing yourself in a particular area. Then, as you narrow down the list of possibilities, you begin to find out as much as you can about specifics. You can go to the library; you can see a career counselor; you can talk with friends, or those who are engaged in that activity. You can actually take the idea and live with it for a while.

It's very important not to become impatient at this point. By the time you are ready to dedicate yourself to a specific goal, you must feel confident that you have done your research. You can use the Brainstorming Work Sheet in the Exercise Section of this chapter to help you evaluate your options.

Once you have explored your options, you will be ready to set your goal and say, "That's what I want! This is the way I want to express my talents at this time in my life!"

DEDICATION TO A GOAL IN THE FUTURE GOVERNS OUR BEHAVIOR IN THE PRESENT.

Once you have made your commitment, you can begin the work of preparation. You can begin to back up your ideas with action.

STEP THREE — DEDICATE YOURSELF
KEY IDEAS

- THROUGH SELF-KNOWLEDGE, WE BECOME ABLE TO SET EFFECTIVE GOALS AND DEDICATE OURSELVES TO EXPRESSING THEM.

- PERSISTENCE AND DETERMINATION CAN MEAN THE DIFFERENCE BETWEEN FULFILLMENT AND FRUSTRATION.

- MANY DIFFERENT PATHS CAN LEAD US TO OUR DESTINATION.

- IT IS IMPORTANT NOT TO GIVE UP AT THE FIRST SIGN OF A CHALLENGE.

- EACH OF US CAN BE AN OVERCOMER — THE HERO OF OUR OWN LIFE.

- OUR TALENTS AND SKILLS CAN BE USED IN A VARIETY OF WAYS.

- WE EXPERIENCE TRUE FULFILLMENT BY EXPRESSING WHO WE ARE.

EXERCISES FOR DEDICATION

> ***"Follow your dream...***
> ***take one step at a time,***
> ***and don't settle for less.***
> ***Just continue to climb."***
>
> AMANDA BRADLEY

Based on what you have learned about yourself in the previous exercises, and the recommended reading, you are ready to decide which area, activity, lifestyle, or career will be most meaningful for you at this time.

By now, you know your strengths and weaknesses, your values, what type of activities give you pleasure. These exercises will help you discover and explore your many options.

Before you engage in the brainstorming exercise, you might want to get some ideas from WHAT COLOR IS YOUR PARACHUTE, and DISCOVER WHAT YOU ARE BEST AT, recommended at the end of this chapter. Both of these books provide questions that will help you discover more of yourself and your special talents. Remember to begin your brainstorming session by stating your broad area of interest.

BRAINSTORMING WORK SHEET

MY AREA OF INTEREST IS ______________________

____

HERE ARE THE WAYS I MIGHT EXPERIENCE THIS:

This is not the time to be conservative in your thinking. Write *everything* down, no matter how silly or improbable it sounds.

______________________ ______________________

______________________ ______________________

______________________ ______________________

______________________ ______________________

______________________ ______________________

______________________ ______________________

After you think you have exhausted the possibilities, try to come up with five more.

______________________ ______________________

______________________ ______________________

____

Now you know of several *possible* ways that you can express yourself in your area of interest. It's time to narrow the list down to a few *probabilities*.

Get Real!

Take your brainstorming list and narrow it down to two or three ways you might express your abilities. Do some research on each of your choices. Your local library provides a wealth of information about nearly anything you need to know. Talk to people who are engaged in these activities. Learn all you can about exactly what it will take to accomplish each, and ask yourself these questions:

1. What is it about each of them that appeals to you?

POSSIBILITY #1: ______________________________

POSSIBILITY #2: ______________________________

POSSIBILITY #3: ______________________________

2. How are they similar?

____

____

____

3. How are they different?

____

____

____

4. Write your possibilities down, along with the pros and cons of each. Consider things such as training needed, money needed, locale, special abilities, etc.

POSSIBILITY #1	PROS	CONS
__________	__________	__________
	__________	__________
	__________	__________
POSSIBILITY #2	**PROS**	**CONS**
__________	__________	__________
	__________	__________
	__________	__________
POSSIBILITY #3	**PROS**	**CONS**
__________	__________	__________
	__________	__________
	__________	__________

Remember, much research and contemplation must take place before you focus on a specific goal. After weighing the information you have put together about each of your possibilities, make a choice and write it on the contract provided.

> ***"The world makes way***
> ***for the man or woman with a purpose.***
> ***Take time to choose a high purpose today ...***
> ***then stick to it,***
> ***and you will transform your life."***
>
> J. SIG PAULSON

COMMITMENT CONTRACT

I DEDICATE MY TALENTS, MY ENERGIES,
AND MY EFFORTS TO EXPRESSING MYSELF
IN THE FOLLOWING WAY:

____

____

____

____

____

____

____

____

____

Your Signature

Dated this _____ day of ________________, ____

AFFIRMATION

I CHOOSE TO FOLLOW MY DESTINY. I AM ENTHUSIASTIC, COURAGEOUS AND PERSISTENT!

RECOMMENDED READING

DISCOVER WHAT YOU'RE BEST AT, The National Career Aptitude System and Career Directory, Barry & Linda Gale. 1990. Fireside (Simon & Schuster), New York

A collection of aptitude tests designed to help you determine your areas of skill. Also provides help in researching career options.

FEEL THE FEAR AND DO IT ANYWAY, Susan Jeffries, Ph.D. 1987 Fawcett Columbine, New York

Helps us recognize that it is not uncommon to experience fear, and gives us tools for moving forward in the face of fear.

LIVING HAPPILY EVER AFTER, Marsha Sinetar. 1990. Dell Publishing, New York

Inspiring account that emphasizes the Hero's Journey, and triumph over adversity.

WHAT COLOR IS YOUR PARACHUTE, A Practical Manual for Job Hunters and Career Changers, Richard Nelson Bolles 1992. Ten-Speed Press.

First published in 1970, this book is updated every year. It helps you identify your skills and strengths, and offers advice on choosing a career and interviewing for jobs.

YES or NO, Spencer Johnson, M.D. 1992. HarperCollins Publishers, New York.

A guide to making better decisions, sooner, and enjoying better relationships at work and at home.

STEP FOUR

PREPARE YOURSELF

Talent is like
a raw gemstone...
uncut and unpolished.
It's true value
lies in its potential!

"You are never
given a wish
without also
being given
the power
to make it true.
You may have
to work for it,
however!"

RICHARD BACH

The first three steps in this creative process take place in your mind. They are involved with inner freedom, self-knowledge, and a heartfelt dedication. These are mental, emotional, and spiritual activities. They are the preparation of the soil before the seeds are planted.

Now it's time to take some action — based on all that you know and feel and believe to be true. It's time to plant some seeds. The commitment to your goal MUST be followed by an actual activity, and the beginning of that activity is preparation!

Enjoy The Freedom of Excellence

Having a talent for something carries with it a responsibility. You might be a "natural" at something, but that doesn't mean you shouldn't do everything you can do to cultivate and nurture that talent.

This is the time in the creative process to take a look at what you want to do, and make sure you are prepared to do it well.

Preparation for success begins with an attitude of mind — an attitude that is unwilling to settle for anything less than the best.

Some years ago, I worked as a voice teacher. Sometimes, my students became discouraged, and quit taking lessons, because they were bored with the constant repetition of practicing scales and vocal exercises. Of course, singing is much more than the practice of technique, but only through mastering the basics can we truly excel in anything. Singing can be one of the most exciting and freeing ways to express. Yet, it can also be frustrating if we cannot control our breathing or be certain what kind of sounds we are producing.

In my own work, I never experienced any real freedom of expression until I had achieved a certain level of mastery. I'm not suggesting that I have mastered singing completely, but I have prepared myself to the degree that I can interpret a song without having to worry about my technique. It's an exciting and joyful feeling.

Creative fulfillment comes from unlocking those doors inside of us that have been closed due to a lack of training and education. People who have mastered the piano, for example, are able to move their fingers with a dexterity that makes their playing appear effortless. In fact, when you see somebody perform a task extremely well and with apparent ease, you can be sure that a great deal of study and preparation went into it.

IT TAKES A LOT OF WORK
TO DO A THING EFFORTLESSLY!

Victor Borge is one of the great examples of how enjoyable mastery can be. If he wasn't such a fine pianist he would not be able to have all the fun at the piano that is his trademark. In the Ice Capades, we see the clown skaters tripping and falling all over the ice. They need to be extremely accomplished skaters, in order to perform their antics well. Comic divers have to know a great deal about diving, to entertain safely and expertly.

I believe it is a real waste for an individual to possess a natural talent for something and not develop that talent to it's fullest potential.

Carol, my business partner and co-author of this book is a fine pianist. As a child, she was considered a prodigy. But a combination of burn-out and rebelliousness caused her to quit studying music while she was still in her teens. Although she enjoyed success in other fields, as time passed, she began to regret not following through on her musical talent.

When we know we are gifted and, for one reason or another, are not developing and sharing that gift, we sometimes feel a sense of longing — as though a part of ourselves is missing.

Well, it's never too late!

Thirty years after her last piano lesson, Carol began to study music again. She wanted to learn chord structure so she could embellish musical arrangements, do some arranging of her own, and perhaps even some composition.

Today she is my music director and accompanies me during my seminars and recording sessions. She is experiencing a joy and creative fulfillment that was unknown to her before she continued developing her musical talent.

We all have the opportunity to start right now to do those things we might regret not having done before. The nostalgic longing we feel is actually our creative potential attempting to push its way out. It's important that our creativity find expression because it is part and parcel of who we are as individuals. We have to take the responsibility for cultivating the gifts we are given.

Check the Cupboards and Make a Shopping List

Let us assume that, at this point, you are committed to achieving a particular goal. One of the first things you need to do is to seek out those avenues through which you can qualify yourself. Learning institutions, special courses, on the job training — whether it's through a paying position or through volunteer work — all are tools through which you can develop those abilities you want to express.

This hands-on training is, of course, the cornerstone of your preparation process. There are, however, other aspects of preparation that are sometimes not as obvious. The mental and emotional factors must not be neglected if you want to get the most out of your preparation.

When I decided to become a Unity minister, I knew where I needed to go to school. I knew how long it would take. I knew how much it would cost. I knew also, that I was going to have to prepare myself physically, mentally and emotionally before I went to ministerial school.

Once I was dedicated to sharing my talents through the ministry, I had to get my life in order. I needed time to be sure that my commitment was real, and that I wasn't wanting it for the wrong reasons.

I needed to examine myself — not from a position of deficiency, but from an objective position — to see which skills I had, and which ones I needed to acquire. I knew that I wanted to share Unity's positive way of life with others, but I also knew that, to do it effectively, it was going to take more than I presently had to offer.

Having made the decision to become a Unity minister, I had to face some facts. For some, these facts might have been a deterrent, but for me, they were just points to be considered.

> *IF WE ARE NOT PREPARED TO DO*
> *THE THING THAT WE DESIRE TO DO*
> *IT'S NOT BAD NEWS...*
> *IT'S JUST A POINT OF INFORMATION!*

When I looked at the fact that I didn't have a formal academic background, it didn't mean that I was never going to have one. It simply meant that I needed to set about getting one. And that's exactly what I did!

I had never before felt that an education beyond high school was a necessity in my life. Suddenly that was no longer the case. I felt that a person planning a career in the ministry would not only need to be well-grounded in religion and philosophy, but also would need to possess some solid administrative skills.

I decided to begin acquiring these skills by enrolling in college. I took business and accounting courses, and the philosophy of religion. I was apprehensive, because although I was self-educated in a wide variety of subjects, I had never taken college courses before, and had not really explored my academic capabilities. I was committed, however, and although I was frightened, I knew I would do it.

I also realized that there were ways in which I could prepare for the ministry that were open and available to me right then. I became very active in my local Unity church. I took advantage of the extension courses offered at Unity Village in Missouri. I began to learn and understand as much as I could about the Unity teachings.

I began to teach classes at my local church. I also directed the choir, gave Sunday lessons, led meditations, did public relations work for the church, and eventually became the office manager. I paid the bills, wrote the paychecks, recorded the dial-a-prayer, watered the plants, cleaned the bathrooms, well, you get the idea.

Through working in my local church I began to see that being a minister involved much more than getting up in front of a congregation on Sunday morning, delivering an inspiring message and getting positive feedback after the service.

During this time, I was also preparing myself emotionally. I realized I was going to have to acknowledge my feelings about leaving Los Angeles, where I had expected to spend the rest of my life.

I had to look at how my decision would affect the other people in my life. My husband was going to have to drastically change his life, as well. I had to know how he felt about making these changes and whether or not he felt forced or unduly influenced by my decision.

I had to make arrangements for my father, for whom I was caring at the time, and I had to see that my finances were in order.

All of this preparation took about four years, and every bit of it was necessary. I could not have overlooked any of these things if I wanted to arrive at ministerial school with any peace of mind at all.

Expect the Unexpected!

The path of preparation is not always smooth. I was preparing for ministerial school about as efficiently and effectively as I could, when something happened that could easily have meant, not only the end of my dream, but the end of my faith.

A short time after I submitted my application to ministerial school, I was involved in a freak accident in which I was crushed between a car and a bus. My leg was severely injured, and for a time there was a strong possibility, not only that I would never walk again, but that I would lose my leg entirely.

I spent months in hospitals, undergoing plastic surgery, physical therapy, and neurological treatment. My plans had to be delayed while I recovered, and it was a frightening and difficult time. I am happy to say that, with expert medical help and much prayer, my leg was saved.

During my period of recuperation, I thought my preparation for ministerial school had been put on hold. Looking back, however, I can see that this experience played a very important part in preparing me for the ministry.

Before the accident, I believed that if human beings took responsibility for themselves, and developed a positive attitude about their lives, they would be able to avoid all pain and suffering. After all, since I had found Unity's positive way of life, I'd been happier than ever before. I thought I was living proof of what dedication to a spiritual path and positive expectations could do.

However, when I was lying there on the street looking at my crushed and bleeding leg, I knew that something was going to have to change. I was taking a positive approach to life. I had dedicated myself to helping others see themselves as worthy and wonderful. I was doing all these things, and yet this had happened to me! I knew that either I had to figure out why "bad things" happen to "good people," or I would never be of help to anybody, anywhere ... as a minister or as a person.

I knew that my spiritual beliefs had to have some deeper roots. I was experiencing a "theological crisis." Either I had to find a new way to understand the Unity teachings, or I had to throw it all away! This was a time of great soul-searching.

After awhile, I came to understand that, for me, a deeply-rooted spiritual faith is not just focused on trying to avoid the difficulties in life. It's centered on cultivating the overcoming spirit within us that allows us to persevere in the face of all of life's experiences, no matter how difficult they appear to be. It's about learning to look beyond the facts of even the most challenging situation, and finding the potential for healing and happiness that lies within it.

In this way, every facet of life can become valuable to us. Now, I am able to see that my accident, as painful as it was, afforded me a special opportunity to learn some very important lessons.

EVERYTHING THAT HAPPENS TO US IS A PART OF OUR PREPARATION.

Don't Take Your Talent For Granted

Starting to ministerial school was another level of preparation. I was suddenly surrounded by unfamiliar terms and activities. Even preparing speeches was a challenge for me, and that was a surprise. If there was one thing I knew I could do, it was speak! I found, however, that there are different ways of communicating.

It became obvious that my theatrical approach, as it was, was not going to work when it came to delivering a spiritual message. I needed to un-learn some skills, and learn some new ones. It was a very frustrating time.

> *SOMETIMES WE HAVE TO LEARN THINGS WE THINK WE ALREADY KNOW.*

We should never take our development for granted. We might know that we are gifted in certain areas, but we still might need certain kinds of training. I hadn't expected to have to do any work in the area of communications. I thought I was already proficient at speaking. It turned out that, throughout the two years of ministerial school, this was the area that challenged me the most.

Make It Easy On Yourself

An important part of preparation is to know as much as possible about what is required of you. What kind of equipment will you need? How much money will it take? Whose advice are you taking? Why do you trust that person's advice? Is it a reputable source? Are there other sources? The first step of preparation involves researching all of the possible aspects that pertain to your goal.

> *WE CAN MINIMIZE OUR STRESS BY ANTICIPATING CHALLENGES*

At the end of this chapter we have provided a checklist to help you be as thorough as possible in your mental, physical, and emotional preparation for your goal.

Were You Smiling When The Shutter Snapped?

There are certainly times when success can sneak up on you. Only then do you realize how much better it would have been if you had been prepared for it. This explains why so much success is fleeting, particularly in the performing arts.

While it is certainly possible to get a job, or find ourselves in a desired situation before we are completely prepared for it, I believe it is our personal responsibility to become prepared to do the best job we can.

When I graduated from ministerial school, I was hired to serve on the faculty at Unity Village. It was quite a transition. On Friday I was a student, and on the following Monday I was teaching metaphysics to the ministerial students, some of whom had been my classmates the previous term. I was a wreck! I didn't feel prepared. Obviously, somebody thought I was, but I was a mass of insecurity.

I had received my undergraduate degree during the time I was in ministerial school, but there was much about my subject that I still needed to learn. With the help of Unity School, I enrolled in graduate school. For two-and-a-half years, I took evening classes and worked full-time during the day.

Finally, I graduated with a Master of Arts in Religion. It was an important milestone for me. I gained knowledge and study habits that have served me well over the years. Without this additional education I would have had far less to offer my students. I am able to teach now, with a much deeper sense of ease and self-confidence.

Rocky Road is an Ice Cream!

The importance of adequate preparation cannot be overemphasized. Of course, we expect challenges when we take new directions in our lives, but the more we can minimize these challenges with thorough preparation, the more secure we will feel and the smoother our path will be.

Take some time with this chapter. Re-read it and take advantage of the exercises and other assistance on the next few pages. Find out as much as you can about what it is that you want to do.

If, after learning all you can, and anticipating how the changes will affect you and your loved ones, you still feel drawn down that particular path — go for it! When you "follow your bliss," as Joseph Campbell says, "doors will open where you didn't know they were going to be."

If the dedication is strong enough, there is absolutely nothing in the world that can keep you from achieving your dream. If you want it enough, you can have it. You have everything you need, right now, to do whatever it is that will bring you face to face with your deepest desire.

It's an exciting journey down a path filled with adventure, and once you begin it, you'll never be the same again.

STEP FOUR – PREPARE YOURSELF
KEY IDEAS

- OUR NATURAL TALENTS NEED TO BE CULTIVATED IF WE ARE TO EXPRESS OURSELVES FULLY AND FREELY.

- IT OFTEN TAKES A LOT OF WORK TO DO A THING "EFFORTLESSLY."

- LACK OF PREPARATION CAN PRODUCE INSECURITY AND STRESS IN OUR LIVES.

- PREPARATION TAKES PLACE ON MENTAL, EMOTIONAL, AND PHYSICAL LEVELS.

- THE PATH OF PREPARATION IS NOT ALWAYS SMOOTH, BUT IT IS ALWAYS VALUABLE.

- SOMETIMES WE HAVE TO LEARN THINGS WE THINK WE ALREADY KNOW.

- AS WE PREPARE TO "FOLLOW OUR BLISS," WE WILL FIND ALL KINDS OF VALUABLE HELP IN UNEXPECTED WAYS.

EXERCISES FOR PREPARATION

> ***"The joy of a journey***
> ***is not in having arrived.***
> ***The joy is in the journeying."***
>
> JAMES DILLET FREEMAN

Now that you have identified your goal, you need to make some concrete plans to achieve it. These exercises will help to keep you on the right track.

What Kind of Preparation Do I Need?

A. Financial Preparation: Will you need money for education? Do you need to be debt free before you begin the preparation? Do you need to make arrangements for a loan? Do you need to sell some property? List the ways in which you must prepare financially:

1. ______________________________

2. ______________________________

3. ______________________________

4. ______________________________

5. ______________________________

B. Mental/Emotional Preparation: Will you have to move to another town? Do you have the support of your family and friends? If not, are you prepared to deal with that? Will your decision require you to give up something you truly value? Is it worth it? List the ways you must prepare mentally and emotionally:

1. ______________________________

2. ______________________________

3. ______________________________

4. ______________________________

5. ______________________________

> ***"A journey of a thousand miles must begin with a single step."***
>
> CHINESE PROVERB

Set Your Time Frame!

After making all these lists, you might be feeling a little overwhelmed. Chances are, you are planning to accomplish a lot within a certain time frame. That's okay. Remember, when you take a trip, you need to look at the map to see where you're going and determine the best way to get there, but *you make the drive one mile at a time.* That's how it will be with your plans. You need to put them in order. Some things need to be done immediately. Some can wait a while. Some can't be done until others are done first.

Prioritize your list. What must be done in the first year ... in the first month ... in the first week? Once you have done this, the challenges won't seem nearly so great.

A. I ESTIMATE THE PREPARATION PHASE OF REALIZING MY DREAM WILL TAKE ________ (YEARS) (MONTHS).

Now list everything you can think of that must be accomplished in order to reach your goal. Obviously, in order to do this, you will already have researched your project and know exactly what must be done.

List long-term, intermediate, and short-term goals. Put them into a "measurable" form. If your goals aren't measurable, you won't know when you have achieved them. In other words, don't say, "I'll study singing until I'm really good." Say, instead, "I'll study singing and give a recital for my family and friends." That is a measurable goal. It doesn't mean you'll stop studying after the recital, but it is a milestone on your path. Measurable goals are like the odometer on your car that ticks off the miles you travel. You need to feel as though you're "getting somewhere." Otherwise your preparation can bog down in a seemingly endless list of tasks.

> ***"Only with winter patience can we bring the deep-desired, long-awaited spring."***
>
> ANNA MORROW LINDBERGH

Try not to be discouraged by the length of time it will take you to reach your goal. Especially if you are in your middle years. If you say, "I've always wanted to be a doctor, but I'll be fifty-two when I finish medical school," remember this: *You're going to be fifty-two anyway.* You can be a fifty-two year old doctor, or you can be a fifty-two year old person who never realized their dream!

Do Something Every Day

It's important that you do something toward realizing your dream every single day, except those days that you have designated as "days off." Make this entry in your notebook every day:

DATE: ______________

TODAY I TOOK ACTION TOWARD ACHIEVING MY GOAL BY DOING THE FOLLOWING:

____

____

____

____

Example: I subscribed to ________________ magazine.

I ordered a catalog from _________ school.

I made an appointment with __________.

I did research at the library.

Put Yourself Into Your Dream!

You need to begin to see yourself actually doing whatever it is that you want to do. Picture yourself dressed for it ... in shape for it ... being honored for it. Spend time around it. Place pictures of it on your wall. Talk to people who are doing it.

Spend at least 15 minutes doing creative visualization every day. Your goal must be so real for you that you can taste it, touch it, smell it, and actually feel yourself a part of it.

Our dreams seldom come true by chance. It takes planning and concentrated effort to bring about desired changes in our lives. These exercises will help keep your goal in front of you, and stay on the path to achievement.

AFFIRMATION

EVERYTHING I DO PREPARES ME FOR SUCCESS!

RECOMMENDED READING

BRAIN POWER, Learn to Improve Your Thinking Skills, Karl Albrect. 1980. Prentice-Hall Press, New York

Exercises to sharpen your wit and help you learn to think more logically.

HOW TO SELL YOURSELF, Joe Girard with Robert Casemore. 1979. Warner Books, New York

Helpful tips on how to present yourself to your best advantage in any situation. Not just for those in sales.

THE 7 HABITS OF HIGHLY EFFECTIVE PEOPLE, Steven R. Covey. 1990. Simon & Schuster, New York

This book examines the true nature of both inner and outer success, and shows us how to take advantage of opportunities to prepare for positive change in our lives.

THINK ON YOUR FEET, Stephen C. Rafe. 1990. Harper & Row, New York

Helpful theories and exercises for learning to feel confident and secure when speaking—to a group, or to a perspective employer.

STEP FIVE

NURTURE YOURSELF

Whenever growth takes place,
whether we're growing a plant,
growing a new career,
or growing a relationship,
nurturing is a necessary
part of the process.

*"Better keep
yourself clean
and bright;
you are the window
through which
you must see
the world."*

GEORGE BERNARD SHAW

There is something within each of us, a creative mechanism of sorts, that knows what we need in order to unfold our potential. If we don't listen to it and cooperate with it, we are bound to find ourselves frustrated and eventually exhausted. Being nurtured is one of the most important parts of the creative process, and it must come at this time — while you're engaged in preparation for achieving your goals.

YOU MUST BE NURTURED EVERY STEP OF THE WAY, BY YOURSELF AND BY THOSE AROUND YOU.

What Do We Mean By Nurturing?

Nurturing means to provide a climate or an environment in which growth is encouraged, rather than hampered.

It's important to know that different people are nurtured in different ways. What works for someone else might not be the best way for you.

I once was given a plant. It was a large and lush split-leaf philodendron. Although I wasn't experienced with plants, I quickly became very attached to this one, and wanted to take the very best care of it. I watered it daily and made sure it got plenty of light. I fed it plant food. I talked to it. I played music for it.

I watched it slowly turn yellow and die.

It was frustrating, because I had given it so much care and attention. When I questioned a florist about it, he told me that I had given the plant too much water.

"Well," I thought, "From now on I'll remember this lesson: *Don't over-water your plants!*"

I soon acquired another plant. This time I was careful not to give it too much water. It died! "Well, perhaps it was sickly to begin with," I reasoned.

A few months later, I tried once more. Again, I was careful not to over-water the plant. You guessed it! I buried yet another botanical friend.

At this point, I was convinced that I was not blessed with a green thumb, and would never have any luck with plants. I told my sad tale to a co-worker who, fortunately, knew a lot about plants. She explained patiently, that different types of plants need different kinds of care, and that while my first plant thrived on very little water, my other two plants were of a type that needed more water. This simple piece of information struck me as profound on a variety of levels.

Once we know the nature of the plant itself — how much water it needs, how much sun it needs, what kind of nutrients it needs — we know what kind of environment to provide so it can thrive. Without the proper growing environment, the plant, if it manages to live at all, will use all of its energy just trying to survive. It will never flourish as fully as it can.

The same is true of human beings. When we are obsessed with survival — physical, mental, and emotional survival — it takes all of our energy. We have nothing left with which to unfold our higher nature. We stop growing, just like the plant, and never even come close to flourishing.

THE DIFFERENCE BETWEEN PUSHING TO SURVIVE AND BEING NURTURED IS THE DIFFERENCE BETWEEN GROWTH AND STAGNATION.

Unfortunately, human beings don't come with directions on a little plastic stick the way plants do. It takes a lot of objective self-observation and self-examination, to determine just what kind of environment we need, to grow in an orderly and harmonious way.

How To Avoid The Stress Syndrome

The time of preparation that we've just discussed in Chapter Four can be an extremely tense and insecure time. In order to get the most out of our learning process we need to place a high value on our own well-being.

TREAT YOURSELF AS YOU WOULD YOUR DEAREST FRIEND OR YOUR MOST PRIZED POSSESSION.

If you had a priceless piano, you would take very good care of it. You would polish it. You would have it tuned regularly. You would not set anything on it that would mar the surface. You would do all of this because it was of great value to you and you knew how finely and delicately it was made.

As a rule, we don't take nearly that much care of ourselves. This time of learning and growing will certainly have its inherent challenges, but if we ignore our own well-being, we can compound those challenges to the point where they can seem insurmountable.

Many times, our preparation is thwarted by the fact that we simply don't have enough physical, mental, and emotional stamina to follow through with our plans. Often, it seems as if everything is moving along smoothly until we reach the step of preparation. Suddenly, we discover that we just don't have the energy we need; our nerves are on edge; we begin to doubt our capabilities; we don't feel we're getting the right kind of support; we might even begin to question the wisdom of continuing to pursue our goal.

At this point in the creative process, we need to take everything we have learned about ourselves, and put it to use in a very practical way.

Let's Get Physical!

Today, with so many demands and pressures made upon us, it is likely that we're not sleeping right or eating right. When I say "right," I mean for our particular physical needs. What works for one doesn't necessarily work for another.

There are those who can thrive on only a few hours sleep. They seem to recharge more quickly and have more energy than others. There are also those who can't function if they don't get their full eight hours each night. Some people feel wonderful eating certain kinds of foods. Others suffer from eating the same foods. Take stock of yourself physically. Find the routine, the schedule, the kind of lifestyle that helps you operate at peak performance.

WHAT IS THE GOOD LIFE FOR YOU?

What happens when we don't listen to our body? The result can be stress, tension, depression, illness, insomnia, and a host of other physical problems. We need to follow a healthy diet and exercise program geared to our own special needs, and make sure we get the proper amount of rest.

I can tell you from experience that when we do not nurture ourselves physically, nothing else goes right. Our emotions are frayed. Our mind is not clear.

When I was in graduate school, my schedule was impossible! I was teaching all day, and attending classes at the university at night. In addition, I was pastoring a small congregation in a town about sixty miles from Kansas City, and trying to be a homemaker.

It goes without saying that I wasn't getting enough sleep, and maintaining a balanced and nutritious diet seemed out of the question. I barely had time to stop off for fast food on my way to class. Then all evening, I would be fighting to keep my eyes open.

That entire period of time was a struggle for me. Struggling to stay awake, struggling to meet deadlines. I just kept saying that if I could survive until graduation, everything would be okay.

Many people will give up at this point. Their bodies will simply give out. Or the stress will be too great. I survived and graduated, but I paid a big price — physically and emotionally. I now can see that with more effective planning and nurturing, I would have been able to accomplish my goals with less struggle and more peace of mind.

We can get extremely busy in the pursuit of our goals. But, as important as dedication is — if we don't take the time to care for our bodies and our emotional well-being, we can end up crashing and losing sight of our dream.

Give Yourself Food for Thought

Each of us needs to take some quiet time every day, when our batteries recharge, when our thoughts can be centered, and when our body can be at rest. We can use this time of meditation for creative visualization, where we see ourselves happy and prospered.

Take some time away from your work now and then. Go to a movie. Take a walk. Go to a concert. Play golf. Remember to laugh. Just do something that is relaxing and pleasurable to you. You need to have some fun and do something that is different from your daily routine.

Don't Forget to Show Up for Your Life Today!

Sometimes we are so busy looking forward to something in the future, that we ignore our current experience. One of the greatest ways that we can nurture ourselves is to be fully present wherever we are. To accept this moment in time, even though we may not be exactly where we want to be, and make the most of it.

Many people are so discontented with where they are at present, they find themselves constantly saying,

"When I graduate," or "When I fall in love," or "When I get that job ... then I'll be happy." By the time they get what they want, they can't really enjoy it, because they are so in the habit of looking beyond what they have.

Of course, you will be looking forward, and you'll be excited about your future prospects, but it's really important for you to enjoy the moment you are in now. Everything you do now affects your future. Don't miss any of it!

The Grateful Living

Another effective mental exercise is taking the time to be grateful for what we have. Years ago, Eddie Fisher sang a song called "Count Your Blessings." It was a big hit, because so many people could identify with it's message. Mostly, we forget to count our blessings because we're so focused on the negative aspects of our lives. As a tool for lifting your spirits, gratitude works every time.

Try taking just a few moments before you go to sleep to find a blessing in some of the things that have happened to you during the day. As we continue to count our blessings, we begin to see value in things we have taken for granted. We begin to feel richer and more powerful. We begin to feel more grateful and light-hearted.

Expose Yourself — Positively!

One of the things I found very nurturing when I was in my teens, was to read biographies and autobiographies of famous theatrical personalities. I read and re-read accounts of how these people overcame their challenges and fulfilled their dreams.

These were the people that I admired and wanted to emulate. It always filled me with a great sense of purpose, and a feeling that the odds I had to face were not as great as I once believed.

Who are your heroes? Study their lives. Once you realize they had to overcome many obstacles on their path, you will realize that your dreams are not as far out of reach as you might have thought.

And for heaven's sake, stop worrying! Worry can become a habit, and an extremely debilitating one. Can you do something about the problem? Can you do it today? If so, then do it. If not, turn your attention to something positive that you can do right now.

Of course, I'm not suggesting that you should go into denial about serious problems. I'm only saying that many problems do work out by themselves, and the ones that require action on your part should be dealt with, if possible, or set aside until you can do something constructive about them. Just don't allow yourself to become immobilized by worry.

Choose Supportive Companions

It is very important to seek positive support. We need to feel secure and uplifted by the people around us. If we find ourselves in the midst of those who don't have confidence in us, we cannot afford to be influenced by their doubts and fears.

For example, perhaps you are on the telephone with a friend or relative. You tell this person about an exciting idea, and get a negative response. You might have to listen to a list of all the reasons why your plan can't work, or why you are not the right person to carry it off. This person is probably well-meaning, and is trying to save you from disappointment. Nevertheless, when you get off the telephone, if you're not really conscious of what is happening, your dreams might have been dashed. Maybe it's just a vague feeling of uneasiness, but you certainly know you don't feel as good now, as you did before you made the call.

On the other hand, there are those people whose very presence makes you feel better about yourself. These are the people you need to spend time with.

> *CULTIVATE THOSE RELATIONSHIPS THAT INCREASE YOUR SELF-ESTEEM!*

I'm not suggesting or advising that you drop your family and friends. If certain people are important in your life, and yet being around these people causes you to feel inadequate about yourself, try to balance this exposure by spending plenty of time in a positive environment. Once your self-esteem is at a healthy level, you won't be so easily pulled down and depressed by negative thinkers.

This doesn't mean that you can never receive criticism or honest feedback. In fact, some of the best nurturing we can receive is loving, constructive feedback from those whose opinions we respect. The kind of nurturing I'm talking about is knowing that, in spite of occasional words of criticism, the people around you believe in you.

Cultivate those individuals who have an expansive, positive attitude. People who are realistic and down-to-earth, but who certainly are not going to inhibit you or suggest that you can't do what you want to do. You should be energized by the people you are around, not debilitated.

You might want to attend a club or support group that emphasizes a positive way of life. There, you are likely to meet people who concentrate on what they *want* rather than what they don't want ... people who are focusing on expansive living rather than the limitations of living ... people who are open to exploring and examining new levels of life at any age.

GO WHERE THEY TALK ABOUT YOUR POTENTIAL RATHER THAN YOUR FAULTS.

Your Spiritual Nature

If you have a spiritual life that offers you positive support, you need to cultivate it. If you don't, and are interested in discovering more about your spiritual nature, remember that your goal is to nurture the good that is within you.

When I speak of a "spiritual life," I don't mean to emphasize one religion over another. I don't even mean to imply that you must have a religion in order to be spiritual. What I mean by a spiritual life is our inherent ability to recognize the presence of a power greater than ourselves; a power that lifts us above our self-imposed limitations and brings us to the realm of all possibilities.

As we grow spiritually, we gain a greater awareness of love as a healing, transforming power. We learn to maintain a sense of inner peace, and experience life from a more expanded perspective.

> *AS YOU PURSUE YOUR SPIRITUAL JOURNEY, LOOK FOR AN ENVIRONMENT THAT IS LOVING, JOYFUL AND SUPPORTIVE.*

Listen To Yourself

Don't forget your own "self-talk." If we are going to avoid negative feedback from others, we must also avoid giving it to ourselves. How often do we hear a voice within us saying, "Wow, what a dumb thing for me to do!" "How could I have been so stupid!" "I can't do it! Whatever made me think I could?" Pay attention to yourself. How often do comments such as these run through your mind?

You can begin to change these mental messages right now! We have an exercise at the end of this chapter to help you do just that!

Nurturing yourself is the easiest of our seven steps to neglect. The advice in this chapter sounds a little bit like your mother telling you to wear a warm jacket, and eat your veggies.

It is vital, however, that we care for ourselves as though we were athletes training for the Olympics. It's that important to us. We need to remember not to abuse ourselves on any level. Anytime we do, we are taking energy away from our goal and we will suffer unnecessarily.

Your knowledge of yourself will help you determine what type of nurturing will work best for you. Don't neglect yourself in any way.

Remember, there is no such thing as a dream without the way to fulfill it. If we have enough respect for ourselves and enough respect for our dream, we will keep ourselves physically, mentally, emotionally and spiritually fit, not only to live to express our goal, but to enjoy it as well.

STEP FIVE – NURTURE YOURSELF KEY IDEAS

- THERE IS A CREATIVE POWER WITHIN US THAT KNOWS WHAT WE NEED IN ORDER TO UNFOLD OUR POTENTIAL.

- WHEN WE BEGIN TO NURTURE OURSELVES, WE EXPERIENCE LESS STRESS AND MORE ENERGY.

- NURTURING OURSELVES BECOMES EASIER AS WE LEARN TO UNDERSTAND AND RESPECT OURSELVES.

- IT IS IMPORTANT TO TAKE TIME EACH DAY TO COUNT OUR BLESSINGS.

- CULTIVATING OUR SPIRITUAL NATURE HELPS US MAINTAIN INNER PEACE.

- POSITIVE AND SUPPORTIVE RELATIONSHIPS CAN UPLIFT AND EMPOWER US.

- THERE IS NO SUCH THING AS AN IMPOSSIBLE DREAM.

EXERCISES FOR NURTURING

> ***"To keep a lamp burning***
> ***we have to keep putting oil in it."***
>
> MOTHER TERESA

Nurture Yourself Physically

Answer the following questions:

1=ALWAYS 3=SELDOM
2=SOMETIMES 4=NEVER

1.	Do you get enough sleep to feel rested?	1	2	3	4
2.	Is your bedroom quiet and peaceful?	1	2	3	4
3.	Is your bed comfortable?	1	2	3	4
4.	Do you eat a balanced and nutritious diet?	1	2	3	4
5.	Do you take food supplements?	1	2	3	4
6.	Do you exercise regularly?	1	2	3	4
7.	Are you maintaining your desired weight?	1	2	3	4
8.	Do you get regular physical examinations?	1	2	3	4
9.	Do you take enough time to laugh and look at the lighter side of things?	1	2	3	4
10.	Do you make time for fun in your life?	1	2	3	4

If you have more Seldom and Never answers than you have Always and Sometimes answers, you're probably not taking the best care of yourself. You need to look at your routine and see how you can better nurture yourself physically.

Nurture Yourself Mentally

A. How organized are you? Do you keep a calendar or do you try to remember dates and appointments in your head? We experience a lot of pressure when we don't know what is coming next in our lives. You can relieve much of the pressure by making sure your thoughts move in an orderly way.

Some people are natural list makers and some are not. Even if you are not, I want you to try to organize your schedule. You can buy an inexpensive pocket calendar in any card shop or stationery store, or if you enjoy gadgets, there are several electronic pocket organizers on the market. I have one of these, and have found much satisfaction in using it.

Keep a "Things To Do Today" list, and mark off each entry as you complete it. This will give you a sense of accomplishment, and keep you focused on your goals. It's important to take the time to appreciate yourself for your accomplishments.

If you are not able to complete everything on your list, don't despair. Just move those remaining entries to the next day. Keeping the list is not designed to see how much you can cram into one day, but simply to keep you from forgetting something important you need to do.

> ***"Worry often gives***
> ***a small thing***
> ***a big shadow."***
>
> SWEDISH PROVERB

B. Observe your self-defeating thoughts and replace them with positive, encouraging ones. Your self-talk can mean the difference between a healthy and distorted self-image.

C. At all times, keep your goal in front of you. Keep it, not only in your mind, but also by your bed, on the bathroom mirror, on the refrigerator, etc. It will give you energy when you are tired. It will lift your spirits when you are discouraged. It will keep your mind focused on what you want in your life, not what you don't want!

Grateful Time

After you get into bed each night, make a mental list of everyone and everything you are grateful for. The more you do this, the more things you will be able to think of to add to the list. Look for the hidden blessings in things that happen to you. When you focus on your blessings instead of your challenges the world begins to appear much more positive.

> ***"When you do something you are proud of,***
> ***dwell on it a little,***
> ***praise yourself for it,***
> ***relish the experience,***
> ***take it in."***
>
> MILDRED NEWMAN

Nurture Yourself Emotionally

A. Name the people with whom you spend the most time. Do these people support you in your dream? How do they do this? If they are not supportive, how do they indicate this? Which group do you spend the most time with? List them now.

NAME: ______________________________

Supports me in this way: ____________________

____

____

Is unsupportive by: ________________________

____

____

NAME: ______________________________

Supports me in this way: ____________________

____

____

Is unsupportive by: ______________________________

____

____

NAME: ______________________________________

Supports me in this way: __________________________

____

____

Is unsupportive by: ______________________________

____

____

NAME: ______________________________________

Supports me in this way: __________________________

____

____

Is unsupportive by: ______________________________

____

____

NAME: ______________________________________

Supports me in this way: __________________________

____

____

Is unsupportive by: ______________________________

____

____

Now study this list and decide which of these people you want to spend most of your time with. As we said earlier in this chapter, it's not necessary, or even advisable, to drop people from your life. Just make certain that you balance any negative input with plenty of positive encouragement.

> ***"When one door of happiness***
> ***closes another opens;***
> ***but often we look so long***
> ***at the closed door***
> ***that we do not see the one***
> ***which has been opened for us."***
>
> HELEN KELLER

B. Constantly review your commitment. If disappointments occur, and they will, acknowledge them. Give yourself time to experience your feelings. Don't suppress your feelings of disappointment, but don't allow them to overwhelm you, either. Remember that it is sometimes necessary to take a detour on your path, but you still will arrive at your destination. Seek out comfort and positive reinforcement from those close to you.

When a disappointment does occur, write about it in your journal. Ask yourself, "What really happened here? How can I turn this into something positive?" Keep working at it until you no longer see it as an obstacle that can't be overcome.

Me Time

Make time for you. There should be some unassigned time in your life every week. This is the time when you will put aside your preparation and do something that's not on your list. Swing in a hammock for a couple of hours. Read a murder mystery or romance novel. Take a bubble bath. Go to a movie. Have a long lunch with a friend. Listen to inspiring words and beautiful music. Me Time is vitally important in order to keep a balance in your life. Don't neglect it.

Continue your journaling, meditations and affirmations. A step in the creative process doesn't end when another begins. It is the combined effort of all the tools working together that brings about the desired results.

AFFIRMATION

I RESPECT AND APPRECIATE MYSELF. ALL THAT I DO ENHANCES MY WELL-BEING.

RECOMMENDED READING

CELEBRATE YOUR SELF, Dorothy Corkill Briggs. 1977. Doubleday, New York

Helpful tools for learning how to appreciate the wonders that we are.

HOW TO BE YOUR OWN BEST FRIEND, Mildred Newman and Bernard Berkowitz. 1971. Ballantine Books. New York

A wonderful collection of prose and uplifting aphorisms to aid us in maintaining a positive self-image.

LIGHTEN UP, Survival Skills for People Under Pressure, C.W. Metcalf and Roma Felible. 1992. Addison-Wesley Publishing, New York

A humorous adaptation of basic truth and wisdom to help us cope with many of life's challenges.

WHAT TO SAY WHEN YOU TALK TO YOURSELF, Shad Helmstetter, Ph.D. 1982. Pocket Books, New York

How to make positive self-talk a permanent habit. Shows us how to give ourselves the kind, loving, determined support we would give to our best friend.

YOU MAKE THE DIFFERENCE, Eric Butterworth, 1984. Harper & Row, San Francisco

A collection of inspirational messages designed to lift your spirits when the going gets tough.

YOU DON'T HAVE TO GO HOME FROM WORK EXHAUSTED, Ann McGee-Cooper with Duane Trammell and Barbara Lau. 1990. Bowen & Rogers, Dallas, Texas

Tools for nurturing yourself, even when you have a busy schedule.

STEP SIX

EXPRESS YOURSELF

Nothing is really achieved until it is expressed!

“One must learn
By doing the thing.
For though you
think you know it,
You have no
certainty,
until you try.”

SOPHOCLES

All through this process, you've been absorbing information about yourself, and learning what it means to be truly dedicated to an idea. You have done whatever is necessary to prepare yourself, and now, your evolution and healthy development depend on finding an outlet to express yourself. Not only do you have what it takes to make your dream come true, but now you *know* you have it, and, at this point, you should be straining at the bit to get out there and demonstrate.

> *THAT WHICH IS INVOLVED IN YOUR MIND*
> *WILL EVOLVE IN YOUR EXPERIENCE!*

Express or Explode!

Expressing yourself is not only the next orderly step in the Seven Step Creative Process, but it's a step that you simply must take at this point unless you want to risk all kinds of frustrations. You have reached a new level of awareness. Things can no longer stay the same in your life.

> *YOU'RE BEYOND THE POINT OF NO RETURN!*

It is time for you to put on the mantle of the professional who is worthy and has something of importance to give. When I speak of professionalism, I don't mean you have to be engaged in a paying position. Professionalism, in this context, is not a financial status. It's a degree of maturity and a degree of self-confidence with which you express your talents. This is true whether you're plumping pillows or writing headlines for the New York Times.

You are going to experience a wonderful law of nature.

> *AS YOU EXPRESS YOURSELF,*
> *YOU WILL ATTRACT MORE AND MORE WONDERS*
> *INTO YOUR LIFE.*

Them That Has ... Gets!

As a child, I was told there were "haves" and "have-nots" in the world; the "haves" always got more, and the "have-nots" were destined to struggle. I used to think this was very unfair.

Today, however, I understand that there is a natural reason for this phenomenon. It's called the Law of Giving and Receiving. Simply stated, the more we give, the more we receive. Not only that, but the more we give, the more we realize we have within us to give.

There is a certain excitement we feel when we give of ourselves. The satisfaction that comes with sharing our talents causes us to become open and receptive to looking at life in a more positive and expectant way.

We also realize that the more open we are in sharing our talents, the more creative we feel. We become more conscious of looking at the same things in new and different ways. This gives us a zest and enthusiasm for what we do.

Expressing ourselves not only benefits us, but it can be a tremendous blessing to those who share in our expression. When I feel that I have given of myself fully and freely, I always experience a sense of peace and satisfaction.

Some years ago, I belonged to a church in California. The minister wanted to start a choir, and asked for a volunteer to be the choir director. I agreed to do it, not because I knew anything about directing a choir, but because I was responding to a need, and there was no one else who wanted to take the job. I could sing, and that was a start. I figured I could wave my arms a little and help them sing together. That was about all I expected to do.

Several people said they would like to participate in the choir, but didn't know anything about music. I decided to develop a music course for them. It was basic information, but it gave them the confidence they needed to participate.

I quickly found out that the abilities of many of the choir members were limited. As a result, in order for them to sound good, I had to alter the music to fit their capabilities. I was not an arranger, but my desire to help them perform as well as they could, caused me to look inside myself and find some skills I didn't know I had. Out of the joy of giving to them, I found I could do things I didn't know I was capable of doing.

Learning how to prepare vocal arrangements for the choir, led me to writing my own songs, and expressing inspirational thoughts through music. Up to that point, I had not felt confident of my ability in this area.

So it turned out that, although the choir might have felt blessed by all the work I did for them, I certainly received a major blessing from discovering and sharing areas of myself that I didn't know were there. It was a gratifying experience.

Thrills of Expression or Pills for Depression!

It seems that anti-depressant drugs and tranquilizers are being prescribed by the truckload these days.

Of course, these drugs can be of immeasurable benefit to those who suffer from organic disorders. In cases of clinical depression, these drugs are making life livable and bearable for patients and their families.

There are, however, many people who are being prescribed medications by physicians, who simply don't take the time to discover the reasons behind a patient's depression.

When a person is full of unrealized hopes and dreams and feels as if life has lost its meaning, a pill is not necessarily the best answer. Often, the underlying problem is a need to find meaning in life through self-expression.

Diane was a 32-year old wife and mother of two. She came to me for counseling because, although she seemed to possess all the elements of a happy and satisfying life, she was experiencing an unnamed, nagging, sense of despair.

Diane was wild about her husband, and doted on her twin daughters. They appeared to be an ideal family. She had always been active in social organizations, and in our church.

For quite some time, however, Diane had been experiencing exhaustion and nervous tension. She found herself becoming quite short-tempered and irritable over minor things. She cried often, and felt sad for no particular reason.

An extensive examination turned up no physical problems, and her doctor prescribed an anti-depressant drug. Diane was reluctant to begin taking the drug, and came to me in an effort to find the source of her discontent.

Diane and her husband, Richard, met in college where they both were communication majors. They were married after graduation and Diane went to work in the production department of a national television network. Richard went to work for a television production company.

About six months after they graduated, Diane became pregnant. She had planned to return to her job after their child was born, but when she learned she was to have twins, Diane decided she wanted to stay at home with her babies.

When I counseled Diane, her daughters were eight years old, and she still was not working outside the home. Diane had a busy life, and since Richard was now a partner in his company, and was doing very well, there was no financial need for her to return to work.

During a counseling session, Diane admitted to feeling pangs of envy when Richard would talk about one of his projects, or tell her about some new technology in their field. She had never expressed these feelings to Richard, because she felt she would be disloyal to her family if she wasn't totally fulfilled in her role as wife and mother.

This, of course, is a familiar scenario. Diane was experiencing the deep longing that comes from being trained and prepared to do a particular thing and finding no outlet to express that talent.

Now, I certainly want to make it clear that it is very possible to be creatively fulfilled being a homemaker. I'm not suggesting that every woman must have a career outside the home in order to express herself.

The problem with Diane, however, was that she had prepared for something and then had given it up just as she was beginning to express herself in her field. It's like turning off the oven when your bread is practically baked. You can smell it, but you can't taste it.

Again, if a woman enjoys being a homemaker, if she feels fulfilled, there's absolutely nothing wrong with that. That's her expression, and that's good. But this wasn't the case with Diane.

Diane had been suppressing an important part of her individuality, and her frustration was coming out in all sorts of physical and emotional ways. Suppression is the opposite of expression. It's a process of pushing back instead of bringing forward. It's like closing the vent on a pressure cooker. An explosion of some type is bound to result.

Diane eventually went to work part-time with the plan of working full-time when her children reached high school age. This allowed her to express herself creatively through her chosen field, and also, to be available when her daughters needed her.

As long as you are conscious of feeling fulfilled, then you have expressed. Fulfillment comes as a result of something you do that feels as though you've enhanced your life and the lives of others... even if it's squeezing the greatest glass of orange juice.

Timing Is Everything!

When you try to express yourself before you know yourself, before you are committed, before you are prepared — you risk failure and emotional damage. Worst of all, you can develop false beliefs about your capabilities.

Many times people are pushed into expressing themselves, either by parents or by circumstances, before they are ready. They have not sufficiently prepared themselves, and their chances of success are "iffy" at best.

Of course, it's possible to unwittingly hit upon the thing that we can naturally do well, and succeed at it. Most often, however, the results are mediocre and fraught with disappointment. We are left with unpleasant memories of failure.

Failure is a bitter pill to swallow. It can be so traumatic that we are afraid to try again. Fear of expressing ourselves can lock us up emotionally. It can cause all kinds of physical reactions. It can totally shut down our creative flow. If you have had the experience of expressing yourself prematurely, with less than satisfying results, here's the good news!

THIS TIME IT IS GOING TO BE DIFFERENT!

If you have done all the other steps in the creative process, and if you have done them in the correct order, then self-expression will come naturally. You won't have to push it ... it will happen. As you continue to express, you will feel a greater sense of energy. You will feel the universal rhythm ... the ebb and flow of the creative process.

You Haven't Done It 'Til You Do It!

The architect who dreams of designing a great building might spend months, even years, drawing and perfecting a design. But unless that building is actually built, unless it is expressed through the actual construction, the architect will not feel a sense of completion and satisfaction.

As you see yourself express, you will develop more confidence in yourself. You will gain a new understanding of your importance in this world and of how responsive others can be to what you have to offer.

Expressing yourself in your own unique way will create new and greater dreams; and you will be amazed at the heights to which you will aspire and ascend. So dive in to your life and express the highest good that is within you.

STEP SIX — EXPRESS YOURSELF
KEY IDEAS

- SELF-EXPRESSION IS THE FULL FLOWERING OF THE CREATIVE PROCESS.

- IT IS NATURAL AND NECESSARY TO OUR WELL-BEING THAT WE EXPRESS THE TALENTS AND SKILLS INHERENT WITHIN US.

- CREATIVE SELF-EXPRESSION CAN TAKE PLACE WHETHER WE RECEIVE A SALARY OR NOT.

- THE MORE WE GIVE OF OURSELVES, THE MORE WE REALIZE WE ARE CAPABLE OF GIVING.

- AS WE CONTINUE TO EXPRESS OURSELVES, WE ATTRACT MORE AND MORE ABUNDANCE INTO OUR LIVES.

- OFTEN SADNESS AND DEPRESSION ARE SYMPTOMS OF A NEED TO FIND MEANING THROUGH SELF-EXPRESSION.

- IF WE FOLLOW THE NATURAL ORDER OF THE SEVEN-STEP CREATIVE PROCESS, WE WILL EXPRESS IN A SATISFYING AND SUCCESSFUL WAY.

EXERCISES FOR EXPRESSION

Congratulations! You've made it. You are living your heart's desire and you deserve it.

The exercises for Expressing Yourself are maintenance exercises, designed to keep you growing and unfolding your potential to even greater heights.

This is a crucial time in the creative process. You must continue the life pattern you set up during the previous stages of the process.

So often, once we begin to experience results from our efforts, we stop doing the very things that brought about the results. We stop saying our affirmations, or making time for creative visualization. We forget to nurture ourselves. This must not happen, if the transformation is to be lasting.

Continue to build on your success by doing the following:

- Remember your purpose: To Express! It's easy to get caught up in evaluating your performance to the point where you become self-conscious. You will sacrifice your enjoyment if you are overly-critical.

> ***"Don't waste your time striving for perfection instead strive for excellence — doing your best."***
>
> SIR LAWRENCE OLIVIER

- Continue to feed your soul with positive self-talk, affirmations, and creative visualization.

- Congratulate yourself for accomplishments.
- Continue your daily meditations and your journaling. Let your self-observation be informational rather than judgmental.
- Don't let yourself become stagnant. You are ever the student, and you will continue to grow and unfold.
- Appreciate what you have. You have worked hard to get to this point. Don't ever let it become so commonplace that you forget to be grateful, and are no longer proud of your accomplishments.

> ***"I never dreamed of so much happiness when I was the ugly duckling."***
>
> HANS CHRISTIAN ANDERSEN

AFFIRMATION

TODAY I EXPRESS MYSELF CREATIVELY AND ENTHUSIASTICALLY!

RECOMMENDED READING

A DAILY GUIDE TO CONSCIOUS LIVING, Shakti Gawain. 1991. New World Library, California

Spiritually uplifting messages designed to help you experience inner peace.

DAILY WORD Unity School of Christianity, Unity Village, MO

A monthly publication of inspirational daily messages and affirmations focusing on a positive way of life.

HAVE A GREAT DAY, Norman Vincent Peale. 1985 Fawcett Crest, U.S.

A thought for each day to energize your spirit, motivate your mind, and bring joy to your heart.

STEP SEVEN

ENJOY YOURSELF

The fulfillment of
the creative process
brings a tremendous joy
and satisfaction to our lives.

''Happiness is the full use of your powers along lines of excellence in a life affording scope.''

JOHN F. KENNEDY

The creative activity isn't really fulfilled unless you truly get a great deal of pleasure out of what you're doing.

> ***"This is happiness; to be dissolved into something complete and great."***
>
> WILLA CATHER

Just as the seed that contains the glorious blossom bursts forth one day in full flower, so do we experience the full flowering of our dreams. This is a joyous experience. Our work and plans are coming to full expression and it is important for us to reflect on how beautiful is the movement of life.

A successful creative process brings with it fulfilling experiences in every area of our lives. When we enjoy our creative expression, we transmit a certain energy and zest; we project an enthusiasm about what we do and who we are that makes us virtually irresistible to others.

What We Did For Love

This is the payoff for all our hard work. Much of the creative process is involved in the technicalities of preparation. The singer spends so much time with daily breathing exercises and scales. The artist devotes months, perhaps years, to developing the correct technique with pen and brush. The computer programmer studies logic and languages. The fashion designer learns about fabrics and style. The aspiring chef studies sauces and spices.

Whatever the field of endeavor, it is necessary to become familiar with the appropriate skills. For a certain amount of time this can be a less-than-rewarding experience.

When we are going through this period of trying and failing, and seeing our efforts fall short of the desired goal, we might not be enjoying ourselves very much. Then one day we try again, and this time we succeed, and the next time we surpass the previous effort. We have reached the level of development when we master that for which we have worked — whether it's finally baking a really delicious apple pie, or playing a concerto or building a cabinet.

When this happens, all of the preparation and all of the acquired technique seem to come together in a tremendous synergy. It is a culmination of everything we've worked for, and that is when the expression becomes truly enjoyable.

"This is the whole secret of joy:
being that which we were born to be,
doing that which we were made to do."

JAMES DILLET FREEMAN

Eureka! You Have Found It

There comes a time — and it almost seems as if it happens overnight — when you don't have to think of every breath you take or every note you play or every stage of the golf swing. Somehow it has entered into the subconscious phase of mind, and much of the technique is now done by habit. At this point, what is coming out is pure enjoyment. It's a spiritual experience. You feel fulfilled, you feel transformed, you feel transported to a new level of accomplishment. It's a drug-free high, and it comes out of the natural order of things.

> ***"Joy is the healthiest, most fulfilling of all human responses."***
>
> PAUL PEARSALL

There is nothing as gratifying as the feeling you experience when all of those elements come together correctly so that you can lift yourself out of the technicality of your pursuit and work from your heart. You're now operating from the highest part of you. This is when you know that you are in your right place. You feel as if everything has been worth it. You feel blessed and are a blessing to the people around you.

Swimming in the Ocean of Becoming

I'm not saying that you will stop learning at this point. Of course, you will continue to grow and unfold to even higher levels of achievement. But there is a certain level of mastery that allows you to feel a sense of satisfaction and joy in what you are doing. When you reach this level your path becomes smoother. Your creativity really takes off when you no longer have to be concerned about the basics.

Each of us has the capacity to know this kind of fulfillment. It comes every time we reach a level beyond our current one. So we experience this joy over and over again as we progress on our path.

This is the way it's supposed to be. Don't let anybody tell you that life is meant to be a constant struggle, or that work must always be hard. It doesn't have to be that way.

> ***"I accept life unconditionally. Life holds so much — so much to be so happy about always."***
>
> ARTUR RUBENSTEIN

Enjoy The Chase, But Cherish The Catch

We must remember that joy is not brought about by externals. It is generated from within us. Joy is an attitude of mind. It is not something that comes *to* us ... it comes *from* us.

A dog will chase a cat relentlessly, but lose interest once the cat is cornered. Some individuals will pursue romance and become bored just when the relationship is established. Many of us have yearned for a particular job or possession or experience, only to feel let down once we have gotten it.

We say, "When I get it — him — her, I'll be happy." "Everything would be perfect if I only had (fill in the blank)." And then, once our goal is achieved, we say, "It doesn't give me what I expected it would," or "It's just not working for me." It seems we're so focused on *pursuit* and *acquisition*, that we have not cultivated our ability to *maintain* and *enjoy* what we have, when we finally get it.

The Two Faces of Joy

Generally speaking, we experience joy in two ways. The first way is through the *pursuit:* the period of looking forward to something; of achieving interim goals that bring us closer to what we desire; the excitement of planning what it will be like when we get it. Most of us are familiar with the "pursuit of happiness."

The second way we experience joy is by *maintaining* our enthusiasm once we achieve our goal. This is the part that many people have not developed fully. In order to continue feeling joyful, once a dream has come true for us, we must nurture and cherish our achievement and our experience of it.

> ***"Though we travel the world***
> ***to find the beautiful,***
> ***we must carry it with us***
> ***or we find it not."***
>
> RALPH WALDO EMERSON

An important way of maintaining our joy is by realizing that there are always ways to be more creative, more loving, more expansive. Being a fully-functioning individual doesn't mean we have achieved all that is possible for us. It means we recognize our unlimited nature and continue to pursue excellence in all that we do.

When I first worked in the theater, I frequently experienced a let-down after opening night. My energies would all be directed toward getting the part, then toward rehearsing, then toward preparing for the opening. After the show opened, I had a very difficult time maintaining my enthusiasm. Once I felt I had mastered the role, there was no challenge to keep me interested. So rather than enjoying my success, it became old and stale for me. I felt I needed to pursue new and different goals in order to be happy.

Fortunately, all actors don't experience these feelings of boredom. When I was working in the Broadway production of FIDDLER ON THE ROOF more than twenty years ago, one of the cast members whom I most admired was the actress who played the part of Yenta, the Matchmaker.

Ruth was an inspiration to the rest of us, because she was able to bring an enthusiasm and a spontaneity to her role, night after night. When I left the show, after three years, she was still giving it everything she had, and having a great time!

A few years ago, a road company of FIDDLER came to the city where I was living. I went to see the production and was amazed to find Ruth playing the same part after all those years. She was still great!

After the show, I went backstage to see her. I asked her how she was able to keep the role so fresh and alive after thousands of performances.

"First of all," she said, "I never forget how lucky I am to be a part of this fantastic show. Every night before I go on-stage, I make a decision to look for new ways to express more and more of my character. It's an exciting challenge to look for nuances to revise and enhance. I can honestly say that, after all these years, I've never been bored with Yenta!"

I think Ruth is a wonderful example of a fully-functioning individual. She simply refused to accept that she had reached her limits with the role. She viewed each performance as an opportunity to express her very best, and she found ways to make her performance fresh and exciting, for herself and for her audiences. Ruth had a choice about how she approached her work, and she chose to enjoy herself.

> ***"Enjoy the experience of being in charge of yourself, it's quite exhilarating."***
>
> MILDRED NEWMAN

It's A Wonderful Life

We can cultivate joy by reminding ourselves that our lives have meaning and purpose. We are like George Bailey in the classic film, IT'S A WONDERFUL LIFE. Many of us are living "lives of quiet desperation" because we don't realize our value and importance.

George thought he was wasting his life in Bedford Falls. He spent years trying to get away, and was truly in despair because he wanted to do something *important*.

However, when George was shown how his life had influenced, not only the people close to him, but also his entire town, he realized that he already was living the life of fulfillment he longed for. This realization filled him with joy, and he finally understood that his happiness did not lie "out there somewhere," but was already a part of his everyday experience.

Remind yourself each day that you are necessary; that your life is meaningful; that, no matter how modest a position you may think you have, you are making an impact on more people than you ever can know.

Look back to some of the exercises in Step Five (Nurture Yourself), particularly the one called "Grateful Time." A daily dose of thanksgiving reminds us that the ability to enjoy ourselves, and appreciate the good in our lives, is always within our grasp.

Your Journey Is About To Begin

It's time now for you to go back to the beginning of this book and begin your own creative process in earnest. Study the text, work the exercises, take time to read the recommended supplemental readings and don't proceed to the next step until you really know that you have completed the current step successfully.

Only when you are certain that you have freed yourself of misconceptions about who you are … only when you truly believe that you are capable and worthy to be the best that you can be, should you proceed to the second step.

Each step builds on the previous one. I can't emphasize strongly enough the importance of taking these steps in order. Self-knowledge can only be achieved from a perspective of freedom and openness to any and all possibilities. You can only be dedicated to a course of action after you are convinced that it is possible for you and after you know yourself to the extent that you can make reasonable choices. Without commitment, preparation cannot be fully undertaken. Without successful preparation, there is nothing to nurture, or express, and certainly nothing to enjoy.

Putting this creative process into practice will change your life. It will give you everything you want; *if* you take the steps in order and *if* you develop the patience needed to be thorough in your quest.

> ***"May you live all the days of your life!"***
>
> JONATHAN SWIFT

Whoever you are ... whatever you desire ... you can have it! It's already yours. It's now just a matter of removing the blocks that have kept it from you. I support you ... I believe in you ... go to it! Remember, nothing is too good to be true!

> ***"Not by reaching an end***
> ***do we fulfill ourselves,***
> ***but by reaching 'toward' an end —***
> ***and an end is always a new beginning."***
>
> JAMES DILLET FREEMAN

(TURN TO PAGE 1)

ABOUT THE AUTHORS

Leona Evans Stefanko holds a Master of Arts in Religion. She is an ordained Unity minister, spiritual counselor, and former Chairperson of Metaphysics at Unity School for Religious Studies in Unity Village, MO. She is co-founder and Executive Director of the INSTITUTE FOR SELF-AWARENESS.

Leona made her professional acting and singing debut at the age of four, and was featured on Broadway in FIDDLER ON THE ROOF, and HOW TO SUCCEED IN BUSINESS WITHOUT REALLY TRYING. She has starred in more than thirty stage productions, including GYPSY, SWEET CHARITY, WEST SIDE STORY, ON A CLEAR DAY YOU CAN SEE FOREVER, OLIVER, THE UNSINKABLE MOLLY BROWN, AND BYE, BYE, BIRDIE.

She resides in Pensacola, FL, with her son, Tony, and is minister at Unity of Gulf Breeze, FL. She is listed in WHO'S WHO IN AMERICAN WOMEN, WHO'S WHO IN EDUCATION, and WHO'S WHO IN RELIGION.

Carol Keefer is a writer with an extensive background in advertising and public relations. In addition to NOTHING IS TOO GOOD TO BE TRUE, she is the author of DINING OUT IN NEW ORLEANS. During her career, spanning more than 25 years in communications, she has written numerous magazine articles, brochures, newsletters, advertisements, and radio and television commercials. She has worked as an editor for a regional book publisher, and owned her own advertising agency.

Carol is co-founder and Managing Director of the INSTITUTE FOR SELF-AWARENESS. She is an accomplished musician, and serves as music director for Leona Stefanko's seminars and personal appearances. She is the mother of three children, and resides in Pensacola, FL.

FOR MORE INFORMATION

Leona Stefanko is available for lectures, conferences, workshops, and speaking engagements throughout the country. In addition to her seminar using the principles in her book, NOTHING IS TOO GOOD TO BE TRUE, she offers a variety of dynamic programs designed to develop creative potential, self-confidence, and inner peace.

Write or call for more information regarding these personal appearances:

ISA

INSTITUTE FOR SELF-AWARENESS, INC.
P.O. Box 30131
Pensacola, FL 32503
904/435-0588

DO YOU HAVE THE AUDIO TAPE THAT ACCOMPANIES THIS BOOK?

The *Nothing Is Too Good To Be True* audio cassette contains The Golden Door meditation on one side, and, on the other side, a collection of inspirational songs, written and performed by Leona Stefanko.

It is a marvelous companion to the book, and a useful tool for self-discovery and creative visualization.

ORDER YOUR TAPE TODAY!

ORDER FORM

TITLE	PRICE	QTY.	TOTAL
NOTHING IS TOO GOOD TO BE TRUE (BOOK)	$9.95		
NOTHING IS TOO GOOD TO BE TRUE (Audio Tape: Meditation and Songs)	$9.95		
	SUBTOTAL		
	FL residents add 7% sales tax		
	SHIPPING: Add 10% of subtotal (Min. $2.00)		
	TOTAL		

SHIP TO:
(please print)

NAME ____________________

STREET ADDRESS ____________________

CITY ____________________ STATE ______ ZIP ____________

PHONE: DAY (   ) ____________ EVE (   ) ____________

MAKE CHECK OR MONEY ORDER PAYABLE TO:
Institute for Self-Awareness, Inc.
P.O. Box30131
Pensacola, FL 32503

— NOTES —

— NOTES —

— NOTES —

— NOTES —